DETAILS OF THE
LAKE HAVASU CITY EMERGENCY SERVICES

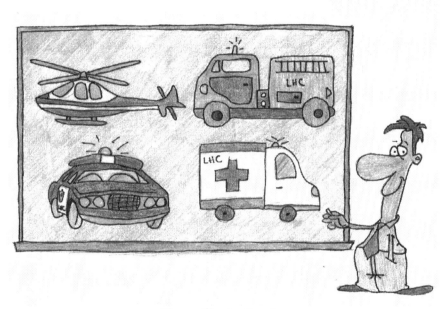

Above Illustration by
Lindsay Plourde

Robert A. Starkey
Havasu Scanner Feed

Contents

FORWARD

Havasu Scanner Feed, a service which I created and implemented, began as a tribute to our local emergency personnel, giving our citizens insight to the day to day activities, show their dedication, and allow them to be recognized by the community.

The local Fire Department saw our offering as their opportunity to bridge the gap between the service they provide, and the service the community believed them to provide.

Our local Police Department embraced our offering as a means of making our community more alert, while showing transparency in the services their department provides.

Putting this program together, I have learned a lot about our local service men and women. This book is my opportunity to share with you a little of the information we have learned.

I want to thank the citizens of Lake Havasu City, my wife (Lizi) and two children (Madison and Mitchell), my volunteer team at Havasu Scanner Feed past, and present (Susan, Stacie, and Gregg) and most importantly to the fine men and women who have taken the time to educate me on how their Department and services operate, as well as have researched and provided resources within (LHCPD: Joe H., Joe M., Clint C., Kenny W. / LHCFD: Tony R., Carl S., Nathan A., Matt P., Tim M., Aaron B., Justin B., Mike C., Ryan F., Kurt, and Joey B. / RMI: John D, Jim W., Brad S., and Amanda P.; just to name a few).

Thank you to Police Chief Dan Doyle, Fire Chief Dennis Mueller, Desert Hills Fire Chief Matthew Espinoza, RMI's John Valentine, the city of Lake Havasu, and our residents.

Thank YOU for purchasing my book and helping to keep the spirit and vision alive today.

Police Chief
Dan Doyle

Lake Havasu City Police Department
Founded July of 1979

Location

2360 McCulloch Blvd. North
Lake Havasu City, Arizona

(928) 855-4884 Administration

(928) 855-4111 Non-Emergency Dispatch
            911 Emergency Dispatch

Unit Assignments

Each officer uses their LHCPD Employee ID # after the word Havasu (i.e. Havasu 191) which they sign into their patrol units under.

Adam units are Administration *	**Robert** units are Reserve Officers
Charlie units are Inmate Transport *	**Sam** units are for Street Crimes *
David units are Detectives *	**Tom** units are Traffic Units
King units are Animal Control *	**Victor** are Citizen Police Volunteers *
Lincoln units are Two-Manned Cars	
Nora units are Narcotics Detectives *	**William** units are boat/channel
Paul units are Patrol Units	**Zebra** units are visiting agencies and extra patrol during major holidays. *

The number called out in front of a unit description, is their shift they are working. (i.e. **1** Paul – would be a Patrol Unit working 1st Shift)

The number that follows their unit description is their Beat Number (reference the Beat Map to the right). (i.e. 1 Paul **70** would be working the 70 Beat)

In cases where more than one unit is assigned to a beat area, the second unit would be assigned the next number in that beat sequence. Example: Two patrol units assigned to the 30 beat would be P30 and P31.

Some calls signs remain with them based on their position. Highest to Lowest: Chief of Police = A1 (Adam 1), Captains are 5's, Lieutenants are 10-19, sergeants are 20-29. Corporals are 40-49.

Specialized assignments will be in the 200 series. School Resource Officers (SRO) is assigned A201, A202, etc. No shift number is used.

* *SCANNER FEED SIDE NOTE*: We do not post Adam, Charlie, David, King, Nora, Sam, Victor or Zebra units within the Havasu Scanner Feed service. Doing so could harm an investigation.

Beat Maps

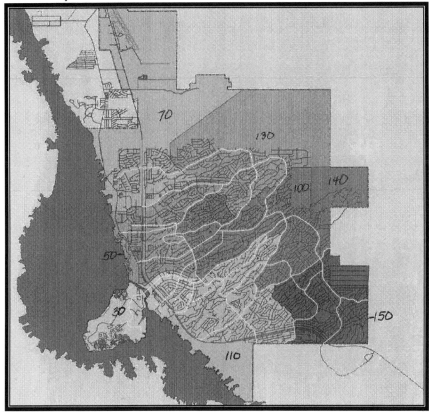

The above is an 8-Beat Map, ideal for when 8 officers are working. So with 7 officers on duty (7-Beat Map) would be less beats and bigger coverage areas for the officers to work. Having 9 or 10 officers working would lessen the area for each officer to be responsible for. The LHCPD has numerous maps, from 4-Beats all the way up to 12-Beats.

"10 Beat" is Citywide, often used by "William" (aka Water Patrol) units.

Police Codes & Terminology

10 - CODES		PHONETIC ALPHABET						
10-4	Message Received	**A**	Adam	**J**	John	**S**	Sam
10-8	In Service	**B**	Boy	**K**	King	**T**	Tom
10-9	Inaudible/Repeat	**C**	Charlie	**L**	Lincoln	**U**	Union
10-14	Civilian Transport	**D**	David	**M**	Mary	**V**	Victor
10-15	Arrest & Transport	**E**	Edward	**N**	Nora	**W**	William
10-33	Emergency Traffic	**F**	Frank	**O**	Ocean	**X**	X-Ray
10-35	Confidential Info	**G**	George	**P**	Paul	**Y**	Young
10-51F	Felon Warrant	**H**	Henry	**Q**	Queen	**Z**	Zebra
10-51M	Misdemeanor	**I**	Ida	**R**	Robert		

10-CODES		EMERGENCY CODES	
10-97	On Scene		
9 – CODES		**Code 3**	Emergency / Lights & Sirens
901	Dead Body	**Code 4**	No Additional Assistance Required
906	Back-up	**OTHER CODES**	
918	Mental Subject	**390/DUI** Drunk Driver	**RO** Registered Owner
961	Accident	**ATL** Attempt to Locate	**FI** Field Investigation
999	Officer Needs Help	**GOA** Gone on Arrival	**DR** Disposition Report
		DOT Direction of Travel	**RP** Reporting Party
		DOB Date of Birth	**DOE** Date of Expiration
		MDT/MDB/MDC In-Car Computer	
		KQ License Infractions Check by Dispatch	
		RAQ Registration History of a Vehicle	
		CCH Complete Criminal History	

MDC/Priority-One Dispatching

Towards the end of 2011, the LHCPD transitioned into a fairly common practice among Police Departments called "MDT Dispatching" or "Priority-one Dispatching" or as Chief calls in his letter below, "Direct Computer Dispatching".

POLICE DEPARTMENT
LAKE HAVASU CITY
2360 McCULLOCH BOULEVARD NORTH
LAKE HAVASU CITY, ARIZONA 86403-5947

December 9, 2011

Havasu Scanner Feed, c/o Robert Starkey

Greetings Havasu Scanner Feed Users,

I recently received an inquiry from Mr. Starkey asking for information about the Police Department's implementation of direct computer dispatching of certain calls for service. I'd like to provide some background regarding this change, and information on how you as citizens can continue to be informed on all that is happening in our community.

Direct dispatching of Priority 3 (the lowest priority, non-emergency) calls via our MDC, mobile data computer system, is a procedure utilized by many law enforcement agencies nationwide. It basically provides two primary efficiencies; it frees up airtime for higher-priority traffic, and it allows officers to view all details of the assigned call upon receiving it on the in-car laptop computer.

Priority 3 and all other calls for service that require a report number are available via another service provider we have partnered with; the web-based CrimeReports.Com. CrimeReports.Com receives all of our reported incidents and publishes them in a map-based format that can be viewed free of charge. Searches can be broad and citywide, or narrowed by crime type, timeframe, and/or neighborhood. You can even sign up for alerts to your email or mobile device based on user-defined criteria. Go to our website at www.lhcpd.com and follow the link to "Crime Mapping and Alerts" to use this service.

I'd like to thank the staff of Havasu Scanner Feed for their ongoing commitment to bringing information regarding public safety in Lake Havasu City to our citizens. We value the ongoing relationship with HSF and will continue to welcome questions or concerns that arise in the future.

Sincerely,

DANIEL P. DOYLE
CHIEF OF POLICE

Area Code 928

Administration 855-4884	Fax #'s	Emergency 9-1-1
Business Office 855-1171	Administration 680-5430	Non-Emergency Dispatch/ 855-4111
Investigations 855-5775	Business Office 680-5431	TDD 855-4114
Patrol 855-0515	Investigations/Patrol 680-5432	Havasu Silent Witness 854-TIPS

E-mail: police@lhcaz.gov

Priority One calls are described by LHCPD Policy as:

Any threat to life or danger of serious physical injury or major property damage. Any felony or violent misdemeanor where the suspect has remained at the scene, or may be apprehended in the immediate area. Responding units will acknowledge the transmission and report the location from where they are responding to the scene of the "emergency" call. Code 3 Response (emergency lights and sirens) is discretionary with the individual officer who will be held responsible for a decision to proceed Code 3. Examples of Priority one emergency calls are:

a. Robbery, Burglary, or Assault in progress
b. Suspect in custody, crime, combative
c. Vehicle accidents involving injury.
d. Fire Department, medical assist calls where immediate police response could save a life.
e. Fights, large crowds, or volatile situations.
f. Unique circumstances which require immediate response.

Priority Two - "Urgent" calls are described as:

Any incident in progress that does not represent a significant threat of life or property. Officers will proceed expeditiously to the scene, observing applicable traffic laws.

a. Vehicle accident not involving injury or vehicles creating a traffic hazard.
b. Burglaries or auto thefts that just occurred.
c. Incidents with suspect information or where immediate follow-up is required.
d. Audible Alarms
e. Incidents in progress where complainant requests contact.
f. Unique circumstances requiring an urgent response by officers.

A "Safety Check" is a check on the officer by the dispatcher.

Department Report ("D.R.")

"DR" is a common term heard over the airwaves; "DR" stands for "Department Report", a number assigned by Dispatch to Police and Fire for their calls to provide internal tracking.

Field Investigation Card ("F.I.")

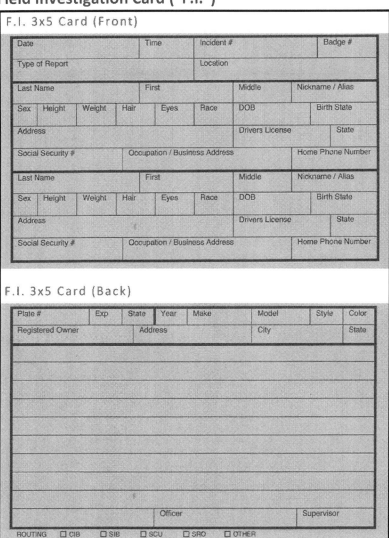

Red Card/Alarm Notification

Lake Havasu City Police Department
2360 McCulloch Boulevard North
Lake Havasu City, Arizona 86403
(928) 855-1171

On _____ at _____ hours the Lake Havasu City Police Department responded to a security alarm at this address, _____.

☐ The Alarm activation appears to have been false. No evidence of forced entry is evident.

☐ The _____ was found unsecured, but no indication of forced entry is apparent. Please contact the Police Department if you discover items missing or evidence of entry.

☐ Other _____

See reverse for *False Alarm Reduction Plan* explanation.

PD-PAT-149 (05-02)

FRONT

The Lake Havasu City Police Department has implemented a *False Alarm Reduction Plan* to reduce the number of repetitive false security alarms in Lake Havasu City. False security alarms not only reduce the effectiveness of security alarms by creating apathy, but directly affect the police officer's ability to respond to legitimate calls for service in a timely manner.

In order to reduce the number of false security alarms and hold alarm owners accountable for repetitive false alarms, the following fee schedule has been implemented:

First & second false alarm in a 12-month calendar year period	No Charge
Third alarm in a 12-month calendar year period	$ 40.00
Fourth alarm in a 12-month calendar year period	$ 80.00
Fifth and subsequent alarm in a 12-month calendar year period	$100.00

Police false alarm means the activation of an alarm eliciting a response by police department personnel when a situation requiring said response does not exist. It does not include activation for testing purposes when the police department is given sufficient warning of such testing. If an alarm response is cancelled, resulting in police department personnel not reaching the premises, the activation shall not be considered a false alarm.

Questions regarding the *False Alarm Reduction Plan* should be directed to the Lake Havasu City Police Department at (928) 855-1171.

BACK

Red Tag/Vehicle Removal Notification

Ever seen a vehicle off to the side of the road broke down? If the car is not a hazard or blocking traffic, etc – this provides an order to the registered owner to remove the vehicle within 48 hours or the vehicle will be towed. Officers' complete standard registration and VIN verification to ensure the vehicle isn't stolen. If the Registered Owner (RO) has a number listed in the Department's Database, officers will often attempt to contact seeking additional information to be of assistance.

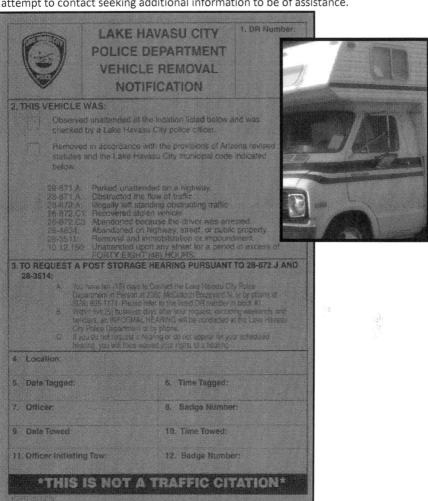

Despite the name, the color of this form is typically a bright orange.

LAKE HAVASU CITY POLICE DEPARTMENT
WITNESS/DRIVER STATEMENT

DR Number:	Date:	Officer:

Print Your Full Name:

Current Mailing Address:

Business Address:

Home Phone:	Business Phone:
Date of Birth:	Social Security Number:

What were you doing prior to the accident, and what called your attention to the accident (breaking glass, tires skidding, etc.)?

How far away from the accident were you when it occurred?

What was your speed and direction of travel?

How many vehicles were involved?

What was the condition of the road (dry, wet, gravel, etc.)?

What were the weather conditions at the time (clear, high wind, dusty, etc.)?

Identify the vehicles involved by make and color.		
Vehicle #1:	Vehicle #2:	Vehicle #3:

Identify individuals by name or a brief description (height, weight, color of clothing, etc.):

PD-PAT-127 1/2 (10-97)

Private Property Accident Report

LAKE HAVASU CITY POLICE DEPARTMENT
PRIVATE PROPERTY
ACCIDENT REPORT

Dr Number:		Date:		Time:

Officer/Badge Number:	Location:

UNIT 1 ACTION:	☐ ENTERING PARKING POSITION ☐ LEAVING PARKING POSITION ☐ STOPPED IN PARKING AISLE	☐ GOING STRAIGHT AHEAD ☐ BACKING ☐ OTHER	☐ PROPERLY PARKED ☐ IMPROPERLY PARKED ☐ FIXED OBJECT

Driver:		Address:	

Date of Birth:	Drivers License Number:		State:	Phone Number:

Make:	Model:	Year:	Plate:		State:

Insurance Co:	Policy Number:	Eff. Date/Exp. Date	Phone Number:

UNIT 2 ACTION:	☐ ENTERING PARKING POSITION ☐ LEAVING PARKING POSITION ☐ STOPPED IN PARKING AISLE	☐ GOING STRAIGHT AHEAD ☐ BACKING ☐ OTHER	☐ PROPERLY PARKED ☐ IMPROPERLY PARKED ☐ FIXED OBJECT

Driver:		Address:	

Date of Birth:	Drivers License Number:		State:	Phone Number:

Make:	Model:	Year:	Plate:		State:

Insurance Co:	Policy Number:	Eff. Date/Exp. Date:	Phone Number:

Property Damaged:	Owner:	Address:	Phone Number:

PD-PAT-411 (02/06)   WHITE: CASE FILE   YELLOW: UNIT 1   PINK: UNIT 2

Citation

LAKE HAVASU CITY
POLICE DEPARTMENT

Complaint	SSN			Military	☐ Accident ☐ Fatality		☐ Commercial ☐ Haz. Material	Agency Use as Report Number
118756								

Driver's License Number		State	Class		Endorsements		Agency Use
				M H N P T X D		

DEFENDENT	First		Middle		Last

Residential Address / Mailing		City		State	ZIP	Telephone

Sex	Weight	Height	Eyes	Hair	Origin		Restrictions

Business Address		City		State	ZIP	Telephone

VEHICLE	Color		Year	Make		Model		Style		License Plate		State	Expiration

Registered Owner		Address		Vehicle Identification Number

ON	Month	Day	Year	Time	AM PM	SPEED	Approx	Posted	R&P	Speed Measurement Device	Direction of Travel
AT	Location									Area	District

the defendant committed the following:

	Section	ARS CC	Violation				Domestic Violence Case ☐	☐ Criminal ☐ Criminal Traffic
A	Docket Number		Disp. Codes	Date of Disposition	Sanction			☐ Municipal Code ☐ Civil Traffic ☐ Petty Offense
B	Section	ARS CC	Violation				Domestic Violence Case ☐	☐ Criminal ☐ Criminal Traffic
	Docket Number		Disp. Codes	Date of Disposition	Sanction			☐ Municipal Code ☐ Civil Traffic ☐ Petty Offense
C	Section	ARS CC	Violation				Domestic Violence Case ☐	☐ Criminal ☐ Criminal Traffic
	Docket Number		Disp. Codes	Date of Disposition	Sanction			☐ Municipal Code ☐ Civil Traffic ☐ Petty Offense
D	Section	ARS CC	Violation				Domestic Violence Case ☐	☐ Criminal ☐ Criminal Traffic
	Docket Number		Disp. Codes	Date of Disposition	Sanction			☐ Municipal Code ☐ Civil Traffic ☐ Petty Offense
E	Section	ARS CC	Violation				Domestic Violence Case ☐	☐ Criminal ☐ Criminal Traffic
	Docket Number		Disp. Codes	Date of Disposition	Sanction			☐ Municipal Code ☐ Civil Traffic ☐ Petty Offense

You must appear at:

Judge:	LHC Magistrate / Justice Court	Precinct: LHC
Address:	2001 College Drive	Telephone: (928) 453-0705
City:	Lake Havasu City	Arizona Zip: 86404

Court Number: 0844-M 0804-J

☐ With parent

at the date and time indicated

Month	Day	Year	Time	AM PM

CRIMINAL ☐ Without admitting guilt, I promise to appear as directed herein.
CIVIL ☐ Without admitting responsibility, I acknowledge receipt of this complaint.

VICTIM? ☐   VICTIM NOTIFIED? ☐

I certify upon reasonable grounds, I believe the person named above committed the acts described and I have served a copy of this complaint upon the defendant.

X _____

Complainant _____ PIN _____

Agency Use

POB _____

ORIGINAL COMPLAINT

Arrest Report

LAKE HAVASU CITY POLICE DEPARTMENT
ARREST REPORT

DR. NO.	ARREST NO.	BOOKING NO.	☐ ADULT ☐ JUVENILE

F — ARRESTEE INFORMATION

1. LAST NAME	FIRST	MIDDLE

2. DATE OF BIRTH	3. AGE	4. SOCIAL SECURITY NUMBER	5. ALIAS NAMES

6. HOME ADDRESS	7. HOME PHONE	8. DRIVERS LICENSE NO./STATE

9. OCCUPATION/EMPLOYER NAME/NAME OF SCHOOL (IF STUDENT)	10. EMPLOYER ADDRESS/PHONE	11. RESIDENCY 1. LAKE HAVASU 4. CALIFORNIA 2. MOHAVE CO. 5. OUT OF STATE 3. ARIZONA 6. TRANSIENT

12. RACE 1. WHITE 4. AMERICAN INDIAN/ 2. BLACK ALASKAN NATIVE 3. HISPANIC 5. ORIENTAL/ASIAN	13. SEX 1. MALE 2. FEMALE	14. HEIGHT	15. WEIGHT	16. HAIR COLOR 1. BALD 4. BROWN 7. RED 9. WHITE 2. BLACK 5. GREY 8. SALT/ 10. OTHER 3. BLOND 6. MIXED PEPPER

17. EYE COLOR 1. BLACK 4. GRAY 2. BLUE 5. GREEN 3. BROWN 6. HAZEL	18. GLASSES 1. YES 2. NO	19. HAIR LENGTH 1. BALD 4. SHORT 2. LONG 5. THIN 3. MEDIUM	20. HAIR STYLE 1. AFRO 4. CREW CUT 7. TAIL 2. BALD 5. MOHAWK 8. WAVY/CURLY 3. BALD ON TOP 6. STRAIGHT 9. OTHER

21. FACIAL HAIR 1. BEARD/GOATEE 4. GOATEE ONLY 7. STUBBLE 2. BEARD/MUSTACHE 5. MUSTACHE ONLY 8. NO FACIAL 3. BEARD ONLY 6. SIDEBURNS HAIR	22. COMPLEXION 1. ACNE 4. FAIR 2. ALBINO 5. MEDIUM 3. DARK	23. BUILD 1. AVERAGE 4. MUSCULAR 7. THIN 2. LARGE 5. OBESE 3. MEDIUM 6. SMALL

24. TEETH 1. BRACES 4. FALSE 7. MISSING 2. BROKEN 5. GOLD 8. NORMAL 3. CROOKED 6. IRREGULAR 9. SILVER	25. SPEECH/VOICE 1. ACCENT/ 3. GRUFF 6. NORMAL FOREIGN 4. LOUD 7. SOFT SPOKEN 2. CONFUSED 5. MUTE 8. OTHER	26. U.S. CITIZENSHIP (IF NO, WHERE) 1. YES 2. NO

27. DESCRIBE ANY SCARS/BODY MARKS OR DISFIGUREMENTS/TATTOOS/BODY PIERCINGS, ETC.	28. CAUTION/HAZARD 1. CARRIES FIREARMS 4. VIOLENT 2. CARRIES KNIVES NATURE 3. KNOWN FELON

29. ADDITIONAL DESCRIPTION (CLOTHING, ETC.)

30. BIRTHPLACE	31. VICTIM NOTIFIED OF APPEARANCE? ☐ YES ☐ NO	32. APPEARANCE DATE/TIME	33. OFFICER NAME AND NUMBER

G — ARREST INFORMATION

1. DATE OF ARREST	2. TIME OF ARREST	3. LOCATION OF OFFENSE

4. LOCATION OF ARREST	5. ALCOHOL INFLUENCE? 1. YES 2. NO	6. DRUG INFLUENCE? 1. YES 2. NO	7. ALCOHOL TEST? 1. YES 2. NO	8. BAC %

9. ARRESTING OFFICER NAME AND NUMBER	10. ASSISTING OFFICER NAME AND NUMBER	11. SUPERVISOR APPROVING ARREST

H — CHARGE INFORMATION

1. CODE	2. COMPLAINT/WARRANT	3. COURT	4. CODE	5. COMPLAINT/WARRANT	6. COURT
7. WRITTEN DESCRIPTION OF CHARGE		8. M/F	9. WRITTEN DESCRIPTION OF CHARGE		10. M/F
11. CODE	12. COMPLAINT/WARRANT	13. COURT	14. CODE	15. COMPLAINT/WARRANT	16. COURT
17. WRITTEN DESCRIPTION OF CHARGE		18. M/F	19. WRITTEN DESCRIPTION OF CHARGE		20. M/F

I — DOMESTIC VIOLENCE

1. RELATIONSHIP TO VICTIM 2. BROTHER/SISTER 8. EX-SPOUSE 15. PARENT 16. STEPPARENT 4. CHILD 10. GRANDCHILD 5. CO-HABITANT 11. GRANDPARENT 16. SPOUSE 17. STEPCHILD

2. ARREST MADE 1. AT SCENE 2. RESULT OF FOLLOW UP	3. CHILDREN PRESENT? 1. YES 2. NO	4. ALCOHOL INVOLVED? 1. YES 2. NO	5. DRUGS INVOLVED? 1. YES 2. NO	6. WEAPON SEIZED? 1. YES 2. NO

J — DRUG INFORMATION

1. DRUG ACTIVITY (MULT. CHOICE) 1. BUY 4. MANUF/CULTIVATE 7. SMUGGLE 10. OTHER 2. DELIVER 5. POSSESS 8. TRAFFIC 3. DISPENSE 6. SELL 9. USE	2. QUAN	3. UNITS (MULT. CHOICE) 1. GRAM 4. OUNCE 7. LITER 2. MILLIGRAM 5. POUND 8. MILLILITER 3. KILOGRAM 6. TON 9. DOSE

4. DRUG TYPE (MULT. CHOICE) 1. BARBITUATES 4. HASHISH 7. MARIJUANA 10. PRESCRIPTION 13. UNKNOWN 2. COCAINE 5. HEROIN 8. METHAMPHETAMINE 11. SYNTHETIC 3. HALLUCINOGEN 6. LSD/ACID 9. OPIUM 12. OTHER

K — BOOKING INFORMATION

1. DATE BOOKED	2. TIME BOOKED	3. SEARCHED BY	4. JAILOR	5. LIST ANY SPECIAL NEEDS

6. HOW RELEASED 1. BOND POSTED 3. CHARGES DROPPED 6. PENDING LONG FORM COMPLAINT 9. TRANSFERRED TO CRRYS 12. TURNED OVER TO 2. BOOKED, CITED AND 4. CITED AND RELEASED 7. REFERRED TO JUV. PROBATION 10. TRANSFERRED TO JUVENILE DETENTION BORDER PATROL RELEASED 5. ORDERED BY JUDGE 8. TRANSFERRED TO COUNTY JAIL 11. TURNED OVER TO ANOTHER AGENCY 13. OTHER

7. RELEASED TO LAST NAME	FIRST	MIDDLE	8. DATE OF BIRTH

9. ADDRESS/CITY/STATE/ZIP	10. PHONE

11. RELATIONSHIP TO ARRESTEE 2. BROTHER/SISTER 5. CO-HABITANT 8. EX-SPOUSE 11. GRANDPARENT 16. SPOUSE 23. OTHER 3. BOYFRIEND/GIRLFRIEND 6. EMPLOYEE 9. FRIEND 12. IN-LAW 17. STEPCHILD 4. CHILD 7. EMPLOYER 10. GRANDCHILD 15. PARENT 18. STEPPARENT

12. RELEASED BY	13. RELEASED DATE/TIME

PD-PAT-106 1 / 2 (02/01)

BUSINESS CHECK PROCESS

1. SERGEANTS AND LIEUTENANTS	A. Review log book for previous contacts
	B. Officer contacts business
	C. Officer fills out the "Business Contact Report" form
	D. Sergeants review officer-completed forms
	E. The form is placed in the lieutenant's basket
2. LIEUTENANTS	A. Lieutenant will review the form
	B. If follow-up is necessary, a copy will be forwarded for action
	C. Original form is given to Patrol secretary
3. PATROL SECRETARY	A. Determine if follow-up is necessary; if so, place copy in suspense file
	B. If no follow-up is necessary, go to Step 5
	C. Forward suspended forms to appropriate lieutenant
4. LIEUTENANTS	A. Ensure that appropriate follow-up action has been completed
	B. Complete the Action Taken block of the form
	C. Send completed form back to the Patrol secretary
5. PATROL SECRETARY	A. Forward a copy to the captain
	B. Update database
	C. Update binder
	D. Prepare and submit a monthly recap to captain & lieutenants

10/31/08
Rev: 11/15/02

LAKE HAVASU CITY POLICE DEPARTMENT
BUSINESS CONTACT REPORT

Business Name:	Contact Date:
Business Location:	Phone No.:
Contact Person:	Title:

BUSINESS OWNER CONCERNS/COMMENTS

Document Any Problems or Statements Made:

Officer:	Sergeant:	Date:

REVIEW & FOLLOW-UP

Copies Forwarded To: 1. _____ Date: _____
2. _____ Date: _____
3. _____ Date: _____

Comments:

Lieutenant Review:	Date:

Patrol Secretary Checklist:	Follow-up needed ☐ No ☐ Yes ⟶	Follow-up Date:
	☐ Copy to Captains	
	☐ Data Entry ☐ Update Binder	

ACTION TAKEN

Forwarded for Follow-up Disposition To:	Date:
Follow-up Disposition to Business Completed By:	Date:

Comments:

PD-PAT-131 (10-05)

LAKE HAVASU CITY POLICE DEPARTMENT

2360 McCulloch Boulevard N
Lake Havasu City, AZ 86403
(928) 855-1171

Stolen Vehicle Affidavit

Case/Report Number:

Name of registered owner of stolen vehicle (printed)	
Name of reporting person (printed)	
ID Type	ID Number

DESCRIPTION OF STOLEN VEHICLE

Make		Model		Year
Style	Color		VIN	
License	State	Lien Holder		
Insurance Company			Policy Number	

I, _____ certify that the above-described vehicle was taken without my knowledge or permission from _____ between the time span of _____.

Due to the number of stolen vehicle reports the Lake Havasu City Police Department receives, it is necessary that:

- I immediately notify the Lake Havasu City Police Department if I become aware of the location of the stolen vehicle. _____ (INITIAL)

- I agree to assist in the prosecution of the theft of my vehicle. _____ (INITIAL)

- Under ARS §13-2907.01, it is unlawful for a person to knowingly make to a law enforcement agency of either this state or a political subdivision of this state a false, fraudulent or unfounded report or statement or to knowingly misrepresent a fact for the purpose of interfering with the orderly operation of a law enforcement agency or misleading a peace officer. False reporting to a law enforcement agency is a **class 1 misdemeanor** punishable up to six months in jail, $2,500 fine and three years probation. Furthermore, under ARS §13-2204, it is unlawful for a person to knowingly destroy, remove, conceal, encumber, convert, sell, transfer, control or otherwise deal with property subject to a security interest with the intent to hinder or prevent the enforcement of that interest. Defrauding Secured Creditors is a **class 6 felony** punishable up to 1.5 years in jail, and up to a $150,000 fine. _____ (INITIAL)

PD-PAT-312 (09-2007)

- In accordance with ARS §13-1814 as amended, if this affidavit is not taken in person by a law enforcement officer or agency, the person who alleges that a theft of means of transportation has occurred must mail or deliver the signed and notarized affidavit to the appropriate law enforcement agency within 7 days after reporting the theft. If the appropriate law enforcement agency does not receive the signed and notarized affidavit within 30 days after the initial report, the vehicle information shall be removed from the databases of the National Crime Information Center and the Arizona Criminal Justice Information System. _____ (INITIAL)

_____   _____
Signature of Reporting Person   Date/Time

_____
Complete Address

_____   _____
Home Phone   Work Phone

_____   _____
Officer Signature   Date/Time

                                                           _____
                                                           Signature of Person Alleging Theft

SUBSCRIBED AND SWORN TO before me this _____ day of _____

200___, by _____.

                                                           _____
                                                           Notary Public

My Commission Expires:

_____

PD-PAT-312 (09-2007)

LAKE HAVASU CITY POLICE DEPARTMENT

2360 McCulloch Boulevard
Lake Havasu City, Arizona 86403
(928) 855-1171

PROPERTY WATCH REQUEST

If you live in Lake Havasu City and are leaving town on vacation, etc. and wish a special property watch placed on your home, please complete this form and bring or mail to the Lake Havasu City Police Department at the above address at least three (3) days, but not more than one (1) week, prior to your departure. Property watch will be no longer than thirty (30) days.

Name:	Contact Address:
Contact Telephone Number:	

Address of Property to be Watched:

DATES YOU WILL BE GONE	Date Leaving:	Date Returning:

EMERGENCY CONTACT INFORMATION

Name:	Address:	Telephone Number:
Name:	Address:	Telephone Number:

PLEASE LIST ANY PERSON(S) CHECKING PROPERTY DURING YOUR ABSENCE

Name:	Address:	Telephone Number:	Do they have a key? ☐ Yes ☐ No
Name:	Address:	Telephone Number:	Do they have a key? ☐ Yes ☐ No
Name:	Address:	Telephone Number:	Do they have a key? ☐ Yes ☐ No

Paper Delivery Canceled? ☐ Yes ☐ No	Mail Delivery Canceled? ☐ Yes ☐ No	Dog on Property? ☐ Yes ☐ No	Night Light? ☐ Yes ☐ No

Please list any special conditions we should know about:

Have a nice trip.

DAN DOYLE
CHIEF OF POLICE

FOR OFFICE USE ONLY

Received by:	Supervisor:	Date:	Beat:
Comments or Special Instructions:			

PD-PAT-134 1/2 (08-07)   Original - Beat Book   Yellow - Dispatch   Pink - Volunteer Book

Witness Statement Form

LAKE HAVASU CITY POLICE DEPARTMENT
WITNESS STATEMENT

PRINT Your Full Legal Name:		DR No.:	
Home Address:		Place of Employment:	
Date of Birth:	Home Telephone No.:	Work Telephone No.:	School Grade Completed:

"I, _____, make this statement voluntarily and of my own free will, with no threats, coercion, or promise of immunity being made."

Witness Signature:		Date:	Time:

FOR DEPARTMENT USE ONLY

Officer Signature:	ID No.:	Date:	Time:
Type of Occurrence:	Location of Occurrence:		

PD-PAT-108 (04-97)

Walk Away Information Form

The Lake Havasu City Police Department has a Walk Away Bracelet Program for senior citizens and the disabled who have a history or potential to walk away from their caregiver or nursing home.

LAKE HAVASU CITY POLICE DEPARTMENT
WALK AWAY INFORMATION

Last Name:		First Name:	Middle Name:	Date:	Client No.:
Address:					Phone No.:
Sex:	Height:	Weight:	Eyes:	Hair:	Origin:
Date of Birth:			Social Security No.:		
Clothing Description:					
Medical Conditions:					
Additional Information:					

CARETAKER OR LOCAL CONTACTS

Name:	Relationship:
Address:	
Home Phone No.:	Work Phone No.:
Name:	Relationship:
Address:	
Home Phone No.:	Work Phone No.:

PHOTOGRAPHS

The above form can be obtained at the front lobby of the Police Station.

Those interested in finding out more about the program should contact Beth Ballistrea at (928) 855-1171.

LAKE HAVASU CITY POLICE DEPARTMENT
PHOTO LINE-UP WITNESS INSTRUCTIONS

DR #: _____

Witness Name:	Investigator:

- "In a moment you will view a group of photographs. These photographs may or may not contain a picture of the person who committed the crime I am now investigating.

- The fact that these photographs are being shown to you should not cause you to believe or guess that the guilty person has been caught.

- You do not have to identify anyone. It is just as important to free innocent persons from suspicion as it is to identify those who are guilty. Please keep in mind that hair styles, beards, and mustaches are easily changed. Be aware that photographs do not always depict the true complexion of a person – it may be lighter or darker than shown in the photo.

- You should pay no attention to any marking or numbers that may appear on the photos, or whether the photos are in color or black and white, or any difference in the type or style of the photograph. You should study only the person shown in each photograph.

- Please do not talk to anyone other than the police officers while viewing the photos. You must make up your own mind and not be influenced by other witnesses, if any.

- When you have completed viewing all of the photos, please tell me whether or not you can make an identification. If you can, tell me in your own words how sure you are of your identification.

- Please, you must not indicate in any way to other witnesses that you have or have not made an identification. Thank you for your assistance."

SIGNED: _____ DATE: _____

STATEMENT: _____

_____

_____

_____

_____

_____

_____

_____

_____

Officer Name:	ID#

PD-INV-129 (01-00)

LAKE HAVASU CITY POLICE DEPARTMENT
MANDATORY FINGERPRINT COMPLIANCE

NOTICE: Arizona Revised Statute §41-1750 requires all persons arrested for a felony, sex offense, driving under the influence, or domestic violence offense to be ten-printed at a place and time designated by the appropriate law enforcement agency. Fingerprinting is also required on any additional charges listed below.

CASE NUMBER:	CITATION NUMBER:

DEFENDANT LAST NAME:		

FIRST NAME:	(M.I.):	DATE OF BIRTH (MM/DD/YYYY):

CHARGES		
ARS §	ARS §	ARS §
ARS §	ARS §	ARS §

Prior to your first court appearance, you must report to the Lake Havasu City Police Department, 2360 McCulloch Blvd., Lake Havasu City, AZ 86403 to be fingerprinted and photographed. Fingerprinting will be done by **APPOINTMENT ONLY**, Monday through Thursday, 3:30 p.m. to 5:30 p.m. You must call **928-680-5409** for an appointment. After you are fingerprinted, you must provide this form, with the information completed by law enforcement (below), to the court at your next court appearance. Failure to be fingerprinted and to provide the completed form to the court may result in your being taken into custody until you are fingerprinted.

YOU MUST BRING A GOVERNMENT-ISSUED PHOTO ID, ANY CITATION OR COURT ORDER (for this offense) AND THIS FORM IN ORDER TO BE FINGERPRINTED AND PROCESSED.

The mandatory fingerprint compliance form was personally served upon the defendant by:

X _____   _____
Officer Signature/Badge #   Date of Offense

This mandatory fingerprint form was received from and explained by the above officer:

X _____   _____
Defendant   Date of Offense

Law Enforcement/Printing Agency Use Only	**Right Index Finger** Taken at time of arrest
Agency: **Lake Havasu City Police Department**	
Date/Time of Ten-Printing:	
Ten-Printed by Officer Name/Badge #:	PCN Obtained: ☐ Yes ☐ No

PD-PAT-298 (06-11)   Original - Records   Yellow - Court   Pink - Defendant

What is a "Detail"?

Any officer can call out on a Detail, or be assigned a detail, like a Sergeant has an Officer attend a neighborhood watch meeting. The Officer might advise dispatch he/she will be out on a detail at the specific location. Or if the Officer needs to handle City business not related to a crime; the Officer could say he is on a detail special or otherwise. (Pretty simple and can be used in a variety of circumstances)

How often do officer certify/re-certify?

Peace Officers in AZ obtain and maintain their peace officer certification through a Phoenix based organization called "AZ POST". Like Teachers, Doctors, Attorneys, Peace Officers must obtain and maintain their Peace Officer Certification to practice in the capacity of duly sworn peace officers with powers of arrest. Each year every Peace Officer must attend and successfully complete various minimum training requirements to satisfy their certification.

Such courses, known as advanced officer training, can include: Firearm training, defensive tactics, patrol procedures, tactical procedures, law and legal updates, pursuit driving, riot control, decision making scenarios, verbal judo training, first aid, and Taser recertification, to name a few. The Officers must pass this training on an on-going basis to maintain excellent proficiency in all aspects of their position.

Indoor Firing Range

On premises is the firing range which provides three (3) lanes, ear and eye protection, movable targets, projected scenarios, and a squad light bar to practice in low-light with flashing red/blue lights in the background.

What are the different Departments?

Community Policing/Neighborhood Watch
Corrections/Detentions Bureau
Criminal Investigations Bureau
Felony Offender Registration Unit
Internal Affairs
Special Investigations Bureau (SIB)
Special Weapons and Tactical (SWAT)

Street Crimes Unit (SCU)
Volunteer & Reserve Officer Program
Explorer / Cadet Program
DARE Program
Pawn Shop Detail
Records/Dispatch

Officer Ranking & Insignias

An officer attends an 18-week course to earn their Police Badge. Fresh out of the academy, an officer wears nothing. Then after several years if they decide they wish to train new officers, they can become a "Field Training Officer" or "FTO". Still a street officer, only that they train other officers.

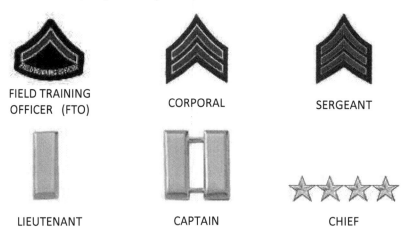

FIELD TRAINING OFFICER (FTO)

CORPORAL

SERGEANT

LIEUTENANT

CAPTAIN

CHIEF

Field Training Officer (FTO) – They are Senior Officers who are skilled and certified to train new officers. Once a rookie gets out of the academy, he/she is assigned to work/ride with a Training Officer – The Sr. Officers, who wear FTO stripes.

CORPORAL – After FTO, moving up the ranks is Corporal, two stripes.

SERGEANT – After Corporal comes Sergeant, 3 stripes.

LIEUTENANT – Removing the stripes, these may appear as regular officers, but instead they wear 1 bar on their uniform collar, these are Administrators.

CAPTAIN – Wearing no stripes but 2 bars on the collar, Captains are now part of the Executive Command Staff.

CHIEF –In Havasu, after Captain, comes Chief.

You will see small "line" patches about an inch long that go down low on the officers' sleeve and jackets – those are called "Service Stripes" – for any ranking officer. Each stripe represents 4 years of service. An officer wearing stripes representing the picture depicted here would have been on the force at least 12 years.

Officers Equipment

Whistle
(for directing traffic)

Min-Flashlight

Handcuffs

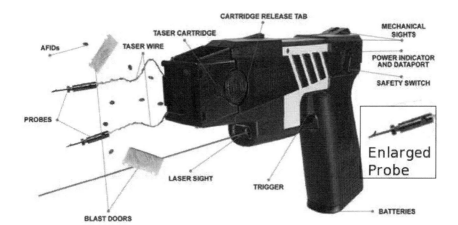

CARTRIDGE RELEASE TAB
TASER CARTRIDGE
MECHANICAL SIGHTS
AFIDs
TASER WIRE
POWER INDICATOR AND DATAPORT
SAFETY SWITCH
PROBES
Enlarged Probe
LASER SIGHT
TRIGGER
BATTERIES
BLAST DOORS

Cap-Stun
(Pepper Spray/Mace)

Gloves

Glock 22 - .44 Cal

Police Radio

2 spare magazines
w/ 15 rounds each

The Patrol Car

Each Patrol Unit Includes:
- In-Mount Police Radio
- Laptop (MDT/MDC):
  - Records Check
  - License Plate Research
  - Internet Browsing
- AM/FM Radio

- Red/Blue Lights (referred to as "overheads")
- Spotlights at ends of Red/Blue Lights bar.
- Front Spotlight (for lighting up drivers or suspects)
- Siren
- Horn

Squad cars also contains a Remington "Police Special" 12 gauge shotgun, Ruger Mini-14 or AR-15 assault rifle, non-lethal bean bag round shotgun; traffic cones, flares, tire jack, first aid kit, blankets, PR-24 baton, riot gear, extra forms, and ticket book.

The Polaris

Even a Polaris is decked out with Police markings and flashing lights, utilized by officers patrolling the beach areas of Lake Havasu City as well as hard to access desert areas.

Sergeants Vehicle
Another tool of the Departments' is the Chevy Tahoe.

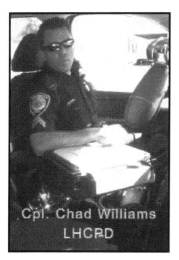

Cpl. Chad Williams
LHCPD

The Sergeant's Vehicle, also utilized by Corporals like Chad Williams (pictured Left). This vehicle acts to provide support to officers in the field, not to transport.

Features similar to that of the patrol cars is the Toughbook Notebook, Patrol Riffle (AR-15 M4), Remington 870-style shotgun (less lethal, Taser only)

So what makes this different? How about the duel spotlights, low profile emergency flashers, and low to the ground for aero-dynamics.

Special Thanks Cpl. Williams for your assistance.

Behind the officer is a cooler with water and ice, beneficial when setting up a parameter or at a scene of an accident where officers are blocking traffic for a long period of time – a supervisor will come around with water and make sure everyone stays hydrated.

A red light on the inside of the back hatch, allows officers to see in low light.

← The rear trunk contains compartments for various gear and basic supplies (fingerprint kits, maps, blow horn), as well as specialized equipment (Riot Gear, stop sticks).

The top drawer is a pullout → easel board to address manpower.

A city map, broken down into numerous beats, is also on the easel board.

Essentially – the Sergeant Vehicle is a mobile command center for the LHCPD.

Mobile Crime Scene Van

Once a Military Ambulance, the Lake Havasu City Police Department acquired this vehicle via Military Surplus, brought it to Lake Havasu to repaint & mark it.

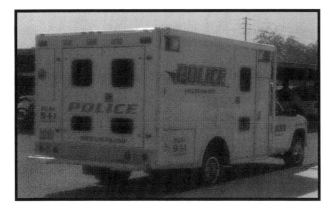

PURPOSE:

- Evidence Collection
- Preservation
- Packaging

After the evidence has been collected, it is then taken back to the stations' lab to be examined.

"Because this was an ambulance that was converted over, the compartments worked really great to help keep organized. Knowing what supplies are onboard and what may need to be restocked." - says *Det. Wilson*

Pictured to the right is a common outside/inside accessible compartment, used to contain different report file-boxes.

Above is a Honda Generator and Inverter [compartment].

← Standard Toolbox

Equipment to make entry into a vehicle while keeping it in its current state; without disrupting evidence or create damage to the vehicle.

Lighting Compartment →

This compartment holds a two light stands for a total of four portable lights that when combined with the Generator, can be used in remote locations such as out in the desert.

← Portable Evidence Collection Kits

Two boxes (one small, one large) allows evidence technicians to go in to collect DNA, Fingerprints, and Evidence in General – package it up, and secure it.

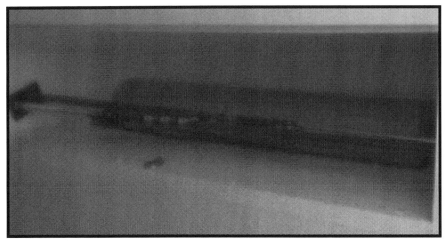

Craft Paper (pictured above) is used to collect evidence, wrap it up and secure it.

Flex-Cam

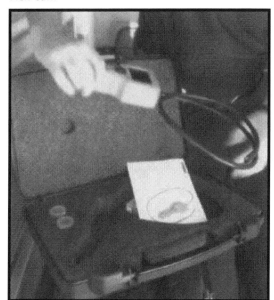

Allows technicians to get into tight spaces, around corners, in crawl spaces – allowing a preview before going into part of a scene.

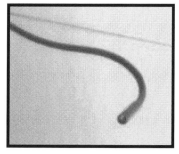

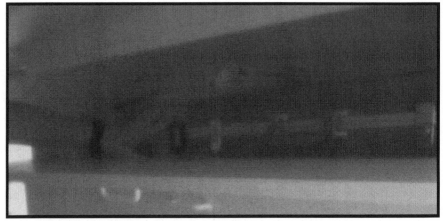

Leveling Equipment and **Lasers** – to identify trajectory (so when a bullet is fired from one known location and identified as having passed into or through another item, technicians can record the bullets path.

Evidence Collection / Packaging Materials

Packaging Materials / Caution Tape

Breathing Apparatus – Self Contained, with a 25 minute composite bottle.

← Masks to protect against odors or airborne biohazard.

← Police Line to keep public out of a scene.

← Narcotics Identification Kit

Tyvek Suits →
Depending on what scene technicians are going into. These outfits protect the scene from getting contaminated, as well as protect the technician from collecting airborne elements.

Gloves and **Shoe Covers →**

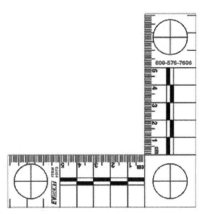

Evidence Sticker

Technicians can take a photograph of evidence (a blood spot on a wall for example) with an evidence sticker next to it, allowing the photograph viewer to quickly relate the evidence size.

Foldable Metal Scale →

Used by technicians when photographing footprints and other items larger in size.

Yellow Carrybag

Evidence Tent Cards

These tent cards also contain the L-Scale, as similar to the above

Large Boxes for larger pieces of Evidence, sharp ends/edges

Cooler with Water & Ice

Workstation for paperwork

SPECIAL THANKS:
Detective Wilson

Heated / Air Conditioned

PD Motorcycles

The Lake Havasu City Police Department presently has two 2007 Honda ST-1300 motorcycles. Officer Joe Murdock (pictured above) and Officer Clint Wilcox are the two Motorcycle Patrol Officers.

The bikes are liquid cooled, able to hold-up at temperatures of 105-120.

Though the State of Arizona, you're not required to wear a helmet if over the age of 18. LHCPD Bike Officers wear a **HELMET** for obvious safety concerns, and also communicate with dispatch and make PSA's.

GLOVES help protect the officers hands from heat while griping the hand break or clutch.

Doppler Radar

Located at the front and rear, these devices are able to measure and report the speed of oncoming traffic, as well as the speed of those approaching from the rear.

These devices can also take into account the speed of the officers' bike, for a more accurate reading while mobile.

Lidar Radar

A popular laser-guided speed detection device,

The laser gun as a "sight" where the officer can see the target vehicle and aim the device. When the trigger is pulled a thin beam of invisible infra-red light is emitted in distinct pulses. When the light beam hits a reflective surface it bounces back towards the laser gun.

In an honest courtroom, any laser reading in excess of 800 feet away would not be accepted for evidentiary purposes since an excess of 700-800 feet the laser beam is large enough to not only reflect the target vehicle, but others around it.

Inside of the right pocket pouch is a camera, paper-citations & envelopes, as well as an electronic ticketing and citation system that can look-up your information by picture, or scanning the magnetic strip on the back of your license to send wirelessly to the printer.

In the left side pouch, we were shown...

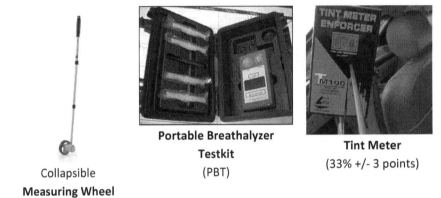

Collapsible
Measuring Wheel

Portable Breathalyzer Testkit
(PBT)

Tint Meter
(33% +/- 3 points)

Not pictured: Portable Flares, tape measure, Arizona Revised Statutes Book, Safety Vest

Adjustable Windshield

Police Siren

LED

Lights

Embracing Technology
TASER's AXON

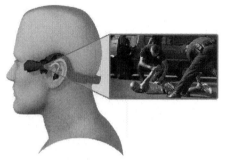

On-officer recording system

LHCPD was among the first of law enforcement agencies to equip their officers with AXON. They are now being upgrade to "slimmer, more comfortable recording packs", an officer stated

Ref: http://m.havasunews.com/articles/2011/10/05/news/doc4e8be79377df8859954290.txt

GOOGLE APPS

LHCPD migrated to "Google Apps for Government" to increase patrol officers' mobile productivity. Officers are now able to check email, documents, and access portal sites on mobile devices. Internal communication effectiveness has been largely improved.

Ref: http://www.youtube.com/watch?v=fBN9HFid47c

TEXT-A-TIP

With text messaging enabled on your cellular phone, enter the numbers "274637" (which spells out the word CRIMES) in the phone number line. Then start your message with LHCPD (to ensure the tip is routed to the proper police department) and enter your tip with as much detail as possible.

Tipsters anonymity remains secure as information is sent to a third party service, independent of our local police department.

Ride-Along

I had the most amazing opportunity to ride along side of an FTO officer on our local force back in September of 2011. Ours was a filled with lots of "Residential Alarms" set-off by the wind which took up valuable officer time. I enjoyed hearing about the job from an officer – learning how they choose their route; and back each other (including the Mohave County Sheriff's units from time to time). You too may qualify for a ride along, request a form at the PD lobby.

LAKE HAVASU CITY POLICE DEPARTMENT
2360 McCulloch Boulevard
Lake Havasu City, Arizona 86403

AGREEMENT ASSUMING RISK OF INJURY OR DAMAGE
WAIVER AND RELEASE OF CLAIMS

As used in this agreement, the term "Law Enforcement Department" shall be "Lake Havasu City."

WHEREAS, the undersigned, being under/over the age of eighteen (18), and not being a member, employee, or agent of any Law Enforcement Department, has made a voluntary request for permission to ride as a guest or observer in a Law Enforcement Department vehicle at a time when such vehicle is operated and manned by members of said Law Enforcement Department during the active performance of their official duties as police officers, and

WHEREAS, the undersigned acknowledges that the work and activities of said Law Enforcement Department are inherently dangerous, involving possible risk of injury, damage, expense or loss to person and property.

NOW, THEREFORE, be it understood that the undersigned and his parent or guardian hereby agree that the City, Law Enforcement Department, any member of the Law Enforcement Department, the driver or owner of any automobile owned or operated by or in the service of the City, their sureties, and each of them, shall not be held liable or responsible under any circumstances whatsoever by the undersigned, his estate or heirs, for any injury, damage, expense or loss to the person or property of the undersigned, incurred while riding as guest or observer in any Law Enforcement Department vehicle or while accompanying a member of said Department during the active performance of his official duties as a peace officer.

READ THIS DOCUMENT COMPLETELY BEFORE SIGNING

PLEASE PRINT LEGIBLY	Full Name (as shown on license):		Date of Birth:
Address:	Phone:		
City:	State:	Zip Code:	
Signature of Observer:	Driver's License No:	Driver's License State:	
Signature of parent or guardian if under 18:	Date you would like to ride-along:		
Date:	From:	hours to	hours

PROPER BUSINESS ATTIRE REQUIRED FOR ALL OBSERVERS

OFFICE USE ONLY

Officer Assigned:	Date:	
From:	hours to	hours	Watch Commander:
	For Data Entry: Date:	Initials:

Detention Officers & The Jail Process?

Detention Officers are non-sworn Officers who work inside the Police Departments correctional facility- responsible for the Care, Custody and Control of the inmate population. Following arrest, the Detention Staff will process new arrestees through the booking process which includes a thorough search of their person; and detained inventory of their property. The arrestee will be fingerprinted and their picture taken. Depending on the type of offense; the arrestee could be available to make arrangements to post bond and appear in court at a later pre-arranged date; or in cases such as a felon or domestic violence related offense, the arrestee will be assigned to an appropriate cell, and will make his/her initial appearance within 24 hours of their arrest.

Following the new arrestees' initial court appearance, dependent upon the order of the Court, the prisoner will either be transferred to the custody of the Mohave County Sheriff; transferred and housed to serve a short sentence inside the City Jail Facility; or released per the order of the court either by the posting of formal bond, or their own recognizance.

Men and women prisoners are processed and housed in completely different areas of the facility. Juvenile prisoners are also processed and temporarily guarded within a separate area of the facility, and are kept away from the sight and sound of all adult offenders. Some juveniles are as young as 10.

Detention Officers are tasked with ensuring the safety and smooth operation of the jail facility. They must continually access all inmates housed inside the facility for their safety and overall well-being.

In addition to processing and monitoring new arrestees pending their appearance in court; the Detention Staff is responsible for the daily intake and monitoring of convicted offenders assigned to serve their sentence inside the City Jail. This can include prisoners assigned to serve a full-time, beginning to end sentence, and those assigned to serve weekends and others, the work-release program.

Operational procedures outline a large variety of facility processes which are implemented throughout each shift. These processes include meal times, visiting, facility maintenance, and mandated court ordered release times.

The Jail Facility operates around the clock year-round.

The Dispatch Center

All too often, the men and women behind dispatch get little recognition. Dispatchers are the first link in the Public Safety chain, receiving calls for service, and sending the appropriate responders, while giving instructions to assist the caller. These individuals hold the lives of the citizens and the responders in their hands.

Dispatchers have the specialized training in communication skills, handling critical incidents, emergency medical dispatching and most important – Multitasking. Their equipment consists of Radio Communications, Mobile Data Browsers, and a Computer Aided Dispatch (CAD) system.

"Dispatch switches channels every 3 hours during their 12 hour shift, so that they are not stuck with the same channel for their entire shift."
– Fred, Dispatcher

The Dispatch Center hosts 14 full-time Dispatch positions, two supervisors, and one lead, operating with three dispatchers on duty almost 24 hours a day.

When to call 911
- Situation IN-PROGRESS
- Immediate threat of damage to property or harm or loss of life to people
- Little or no time delay between incident and call to 911
- Any medical problem or fires

FACT!
Our Dispatch Center takes in nearly 400 calls per day.

What questions to expect when you call 911
- What/Where is the emergency?
- Where is the caller?
- Who is involved?
- When/Why/How did this happen?
- Was there a weapon involved?
- Are there hazards to the caller / responders?
- Are there any injuries or medical issues?

Other Programs

The Lake Havasu City Police Department has teamed up with and offers many programs to educate the community, and the tools to aid in citizen policing.

Citizens Academy

The Lake Havasu Citizen Police Academy is a twelve week course from 6 PM - 9 PM at the Police Station, located at 2360 McCulloch Boulevard. Giving an inside look at law enforcement, participants are taught in the areas of SWAT, canine program, patrol and boat procedures, use of physical/less lethal/deadly force, criminal/narcotic/crime scene investigations, officer requirements and selection, traffic and driving under the influence, department overview, and the judicial process.

CrimeReports.com®

Crime Reports is the largest, most comprehensive crime-mapping website in the world. Local Law Enforcement agencies throughout North America partner with CrimeReports to bring you accurate, official, and up-to-date crime information.

Who pays for CrimeReports? The LHCPD pays for this service for the community.

NEIGHBORHOOD WATCH

What Neighborhood Watch Members Look For

- Someone screaming or shouting for help
- Someone looking into windows or parked cars
- Unusual noises
- Property being taken out of houses where no one is at home or a business is closed
- Cars, Vans, or Trucks moving slowly without apparent destination, or without lights
- Anyone being forced into a vehicle
- A stranger sitting in a car or stopped to talk to a child
- Abandoned Vehicles

Keep your Neighborhood Watch Group Active

Organize regular meetings that focus on current issues such as drug abuse, hate, or bias-motivated violences, crime in school, child care before and after school, recreational activities for young people, and victim services.

Organize community patrols to walk around streets or apartment complexes and alert police to crime and suspicious activities and identify problems needing attention. People in cars with cellular phones or CB radios can patrol.

Work with local building code officials to require dead bolt locks, smoke alarms, and other safety devices in new and existing homes and commercial buildings.

Work with parent groups and schools to start a McGruff House or a Block Parent program (to help children in emergency situations). A McGruff House/Block Parent is a reliable source of help for children in emergency or frightening situations.

The nnighborhood watch coordinator publishes a quaterly newsletter that shares prevention tips, local crime news, recognizes residents ofa ll ages who have "made a difference", and hightlight community events.

Don't forget school events that allow and encourage neighbors to get to know each other, like block party, a potluck dinner, volleyball or softball game, or a picnic.

LHCPD TOURS

**Special thanks to the parents and scouts of Girl Scouts Troop #1585
for extending their permission in using the above photo.**

The Lake Havasu City Police Department provides tours to scouts and other community youth groups interested in learning about their local police department.

In a visit that my daughters' Girl Scouts took - the tour started out front, where they met an officer and were shown the gear officers wear, then taken through the lobby into records, shown dispatch, supervisor/detective workstations and the different departments, the juvenile detention facility (restrictions may apply on your visit), and finally the rear parking lot where they are shown a police car and all its "fancy lights".

Please contact Sgt. Huskisson at 928-855-1171 to schedule your visit.

Fire Chief
Dennis Mueller

Lake Havasu City Fire Department

Began as a volunteer department in 1964, operating out of headquarters at the old airport on the island, now has 87-100 full and part time staff.

Locations

Fire Station 1
96 Acoma Blvd. S
Built in 2000/2001
$1.2 Million in 2001

Fire Station 2
2065 Kiowa Blvd. N
Built in 1994/1995
7.2 Acres

Fire Station 3
3620 Buena Vista Ave.
Built in 1973
Remodeled 2006

Fire Station 4
3270 Palo Verde Blvd. S
Built in 1978/1979
Remodeled in 2002

Fire Station 5
145 Lake Havasu Ave. N
Built in 1968
The Original Firehouse

Fire Station 6
5600 HWY 95 #1
Built in 1994
Occupied 9/6/2005

Fire Station Information

FIRE STATION #1 – Located at 96 S. Acoma Blvd., this 10,000 sq. ft. station, built 2000-2001, has housed four firefighters since August of 2001. At a cost of $1.2 million in 2001, the station provides space for the city's 100 ft. Aerial / Paramedic Unit, houses the on-duty Battalion Chief who is in charge of staffing and operations for all six fire stations in the community, as well as the Public Education Division which offers two public education specialists and a classroom for their programs as well as for other training needs of the Department. Station 1 is also home to one of two Ambulances under the "P3" program (discussed towards the end of this chapter).

FIRE STATION #2 – Built 1994-1995 at 2065 S. Kiowa Blvd., this station's 11,005 sq. ft space was occupied in July of 1995. Three Firefighters staff a paramedic engine company, provides services for HAZMAT operations, and houses the second Ambulance in the "P3" program. Also the Training Division with two classrooms, office space and reception area for both public and departmental training. The 7.2 acres site provides an area for the training tower (discussed shortly).

FIRE STATION #3 – Located at 3620 Buena Vista Avenue, this 3384 sq. ft. station was built in 1973 and occupied in November. Four firefighters who staff a paramedic engine company and are responsible for the staffing and operating the fire boat when requested. The fire boat is secured at the Safety Contact Center at Contact Point. We talk more about the fireboat later in this Chapter.

FIRE STATION #4 – This 3,136 sq. ft station was built in 1978/1979 at 3270 S. Palo Verde Blvd. and occupied in August 1979 with a 3-man crew. Later remodeled in 2002 to meet NFPA standards and a detached garage to house the Technical Rescue Vehicle & Trailer, which carries two off road ATV's.

FIRE STATION #5 – Located at 145 N. Lake Havasu Avenue, this 10495 sq. ft. facility, built in 1968 with an addition in 1974-75, houses three firefighters who staff a paramedic engine company and are responsible for the main commercial areas, including responses to the island. Responsible for maintaining the Golf carts & miscellaneous equipment for special events.

FIRE STATION #6 – 5600 N. HWY 95 (Airport), this 3750 sq. ft. station built in 1994 and commissioned Sept 6th of 2005 houses Air Evac personnel &two firefighters, which staff a paramedic squad to service the Mall, Desert Hills, and back Station #2. When flights are scheduled, the firefighters staff the Airport Response Fire Fighting Vehicle (ARFF) unit, also discussed in this book.

> **Vision Statement** When we enter the fire service, whether it is suppression, prevention, or administration, we are taught teamwork, commitment, trust, loyalty and customer service. During our career, we practice heroism, innovation, creativity, humanitarianism, and customer service. Before we step aside to make room for the new personnel, we prepare individuals with the tools necessary to meet the demands of continuous change.

Firefighters do more than fight fires?

That's Right!   Firefighters are also first responders to medical calls. But here is a list of their job descriptions:

- Drive and operate fire equipment to include: fire engines, ladder trucks, aerial ladders and regulating pump pressures.
- Responds to fire alarms and performs firefighting duties such as laying and connecting hose, holding nozzles, directing water streams, ventilating buildings and rising and climbing ladders; or,
- Perform Cardio Pulmonary Resuscitation and first aid to include: assessing, treating and transporting patients; determine and initiate proper emergency procedures for life threatening injuries and illnesses.
- Rescues individuals by removing persons from dangerous environments or protecting them from dangerous conditions.
- Perform general maintenance and repair duties to include: cleaning and maintaining the facility and the grounds and testing and performing maintenance and minor repairs on firefighting apparatus and equipment.
- Respond to other emergency calls such as hazardous materials, auto extrication, water rescue, confined space entry and high angle rescue.
- Participate in training classes in order to enhance firefighting, first aid and emergency response techniques.

With Knowledge Of: Safety and Survival Strategies, Management and Leadership Theories and Principles, Departmental Policies and Procedures, Fire Behavior and Building Construction, Fire Suppression Strategy and Tactical Operations, Streets and Physical Layout of City, Fire Engines/Ladder Trucks and specialized equipment, along with Basic and/or Advanced Life Support Techniques such as Cardio Pulmonary Resuscitation (CPR) and Patient Assessment and Treatment Techniques.

Fire Shift Schedule

Teams work 2 days on, 4 days off, as shown by the shades of colors.

FEBRUARY						
S	M	T	W	T	F	S
			1	2	3	4
5	6	7	8	9	10	11
12	13	14	15	16	17	18
19	20	21	22	23	24	25
26	27	28	29			

Fire-Shifts begin and end at 7 AM.

Radio Alert Tones

Three beeps is sent over the intercom proceeded by about 5-6 seconds of silence before the details of the call is announced. Meanwhile, pagers worn by on-duty personnel at each station are going off and the same page able to be heard from the device. The Alert Tones are tested for each station daily at 6 PM MTN Time.

Radio Codes

Any Firefighter will tell you they don't use codes, like the Police [did] do. However there are a few acronyms that are good to know.

"PAR" = Personnel Accountability Report
"RIC" = Rapid Intervention Crew (a self-rescue safety team)
"IDLH" = Immediate Danger to life and health. (an OSHA term used by FD)
"BLS" = Basic Life Support (EMT)
"ALS" = Advanced Life Support (Paramedic + Drug Box)
"LOSS STOP" = Time stamp for when a fire is out and is causing no more damage.

Fire Department Engine Company

Firefighter/EMT & Paramedics – Responsible for providing emergency fire suppression and medical services and for responding to non-emergency situations. Duties include: responding to rescue emergencies and hazardous materials emergencies; rescuing individuals from emergency situations; responding to fire and medical emergencies; performing skilled work in patient assessment, treatment and transportation; participating in continuous educational activities/classes; position and operating hoses; and, performing Emergency Medical Technician (EMT) or Paramedic functions.

Fire Engineer/CEP – Responsible for pumping, maintaining, and driving/operating fire equipment. Duties may include: operating fire engines, ladder trucks, and other specialized apparatus; regulating pump pressures; responding to rescue, hazardous materials, fire and medical emergencies; performing skilled work in patient assessment, treatment, and transportation; responding to alarms with the fire company; participating in continuous education activities/classes; and, serving as an EMT/CEP.

Fire Captain/EMT & CEP – Responsible for supervising company and/or sector operations on incident scenes and for the supervision of training of Fire Engineers and Firefighters, Duties may include: coordinating work assignments; comprehending, directing and enforcing departmental policies, procedures and standards; conducting and signing performance evaluations; functioning as the incident commander; inventorying and accounting for fire apparatus and other equipment; responsible to rescue, hazard materials, fire and medical emergencies; performing skilled work in patient assessments, treatment and transportation; and, performing fire suppression activities.

EMT-P – Commonly referred to as Paramedic, but stands for EMT Paramedic. A paramedic practices ALS (Advanced Life Support). A paramedic in Arizona has to have all these Certifications: Advanced Cardiac Life Support (ACLS), Pre-Hospital trauma life support (PHTLS), International Trauma Life Support (ITLS), and Pediatric Advanced Life Support (PALS). **All trucks/engines in Lake Havasu City are ALS, meaning they carry a minimum of one Paramedic.**

EMT-B – Referred to as an EMT, but stands for EMT Basic. An EMT practices Basic Life Support (BLS). Every employee on the engine/truck is minimum EMT.

An EMT works under the Paramedic. The Paramedic works under a doctor.

On The Engine

Driver/Engineers Seat

Firefighters Compartment
Firefighters' Gear and Maps
Thermal imaging cam, gas meter,
building pre-plans

Engineers Panel
Water Controls / Gauges / Hookups

Engineers Compartment
Different Adaptors, Street Cones,
Portable Extinguishers, Foam

> *OSHA says...* Two Firefighters must be at the ready on the outside, before two Firefighters can go inside a burning structure. Most Engines only have three people.

Medical Compartment
Restock Supplies, Splits, Pediatric Bag
two spare air-bottles by below

Main Medical Compartment
"Drug Box", Heart Monitor, etc.

Gas Powered Tools Compartment
Chainsaw, Jaws of Life, Fan
Supply/Working Hose (top-out of view)

Miscellaneous Compartment
Cribbing Blocks, Hazmat Equipt.,
Spare Air Bottles, Hydrant Bag

Gear Compartment

Force Entry Tools
The "TNT" Sledge, Sledge Hammer,
Electric Fan, and Water

RANDOM FACTS!

"Engine 4" holds 1,000 gallons of water.
Roughly the same weight as 8 small compact cars.

Our typical is 750 Gallons, which sometimes can be
dropped as quickly as within 1 or 2 minutes.

I.S.O. Rating (Insurance Services Office, Inc.)

ISO conducts surveys of communities with public fire protection throughout the nation. In doing so, they evaluate the fire department, the emergency dispatch center, the water supply throughout the community, and the level of service provided by each. From their findings they classify the community on a scale of 1 (the best) to 10 (the worst).

As of 2009's audit, the city's classification remains a Class 3, utilized to calculate property insurance premiums for both commercial & residential properties.

Turn-Out Gear/Equipment

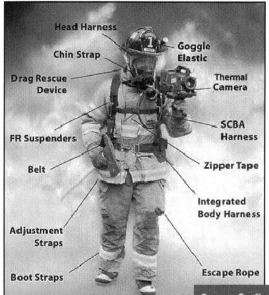

Head Harness

Chin Strap

Goggle Elastic

Drag Rescue Device

Thermal Camera

SCBA Harness

FR Suspenders

Zipper Tape

Belt

Integrated Body Harness

Adjustment Straps

Boot Straps

Escape Rope

Firefighters carry items on them such as an Inner tube for keeping doors from locking behind them, Wedges, crayons for search and rescue & breaker marking, carabineer and webbing, wire cutters/dykes, knives, and various other personally collected tools.

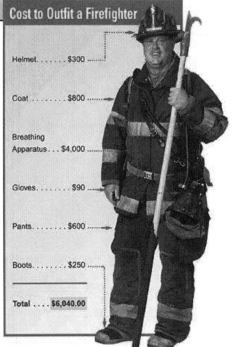

Cost to Outfit a Firefighter

Helmet. $300

Coat $800

Breathing Apparatus . . . $4,000

Gloves. $90

Pants. $600

Boots. $250

Total $6,040.00

Mapping

Below is a zoomed-in snapshot of a printed Fire Map. Seen also on Fire Engine MDTs', clearly marked are streets, landmarks, and hydrant locations. Helpful to the Captain when strategizing a game-plan as to which closest hydrant they will drop off their Firefighter at.

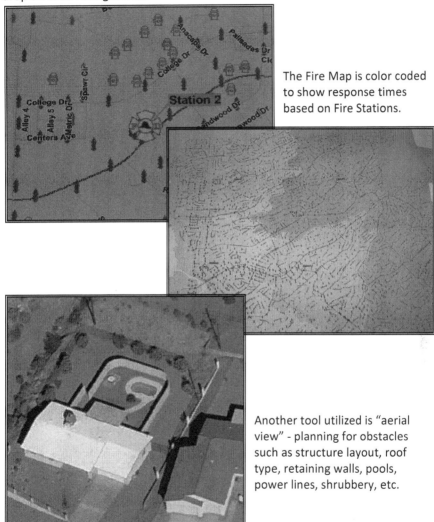

The Fire Map is color coded to show response times based on Fire Stations.

Another tool utilized is "aerial view" - planning for obstacles such as structure layout, roof type, retaining walls, pools, power lines, shrubbery, etc.

Training Facility

A regional training site for the State of Arizona and California - Lake Havasu City houses it's very own Firefighting Training Center (Built in 2005). Used by many surrounding fire agencies, and even the Lake Havasu City Police SWAT Team for tactical training (search and seizure, controlling, and mitigating hostage situation) – features 3 burn rooms for live fire capabilities at different levels within the tower, moveable walls to create a maze for search and rescue training, a 4 story elevator shaft for rappel and retraction training, rafters, confined spaces, smoke drills, aerial

operations, ground ladder operations, and roof ventilation techniques.

A partnership with UniSource Gas/Electric provides the department with real electrical and gas training props.

The property also provides drivers training for other departments requiring a CDL certification.

Confined Spaces

(Left) With full gear on, trainees must take their air-tank off and push it in front of them as they maneuver their way through this narrow tunnel.

Steel Attic Joists

Movable Objects

Furniture is commonly placed in different configurations around the room to help simulate actual living conditions.

Walls on tracks, allow the maze obstacle to be re-adjusted, so Firefighters do not get familiar with the room layout.

Rooftop Props

Rooftop Ventilation can quickly remove smoke inside a room, increasing visibility for Firefighters inside. Here, Firefighters practice ventilation without cutting joists or studs, compromising the structures' integrity.

Firefighters train with several different rooftop pitches.

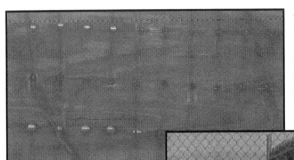

When gaining access saves lives, our Firefighters practice advanced entry techniques such as shaving bolts for removing metal security doors.

Another part of this same contraption built by fellow Firefighters, is how quickly a firefighter can cut through rebar held at different angles.

Garage Fires are the most responded to call by Firefighters around the world. Proper cuts gain easy and safe access.

"Strength" and "Aim" is the goal here when using a sledge hammer against this block of tightly compressed sheets of rubber (shown to the right), or break the dowel-pin on the contraption to the left.

FLASHOVER CHAMBER

Very few Fire Departments in the US study Fire like we do here in Lake Havasu, following the same teachings as the Swedish, Fire Station #2 (Training Center) houses a flashover chamber, which allows a firefighter to see (under controlled variables) what a Flashover (the point of total incineration due to extreme heat) looks like before it happens, allowing for improved safety of our Fire Fighters.

This image taken on Saturday, April 14, 2012 by Captain Tony Rivello

"An example of flashover is when a piece of furniture is ignited in a domestic room. The fire involving the initial piece of furniture can produce a layer of hot smoke which spreads across the ceiling in the room. The hot buoyant smoke layer grows in depth, as it is bounded by the walls of the room. The radiated heat from this layer heats the surfaces of the directly exposed combustible materials in the room, causing them to give off flammable gases via pyrolysis. When the temperatures of the evolved gases becomes high enough, these gases will ignite." **--- As quoted by Wikipedia**

Propane Props

Tank Prop →

← Simulated Overturned Tanker

Christmas Tree Prop →

← Burned out vehicle to simulate rescues and fire control.

MCC Fire Academy
Training Day at Station #2, May 12 of 2012

Applicants to the Fire Academy must be at least 18 years of age, be in good physical condition, be a United States Citizen or Lawful Alien, and be able to pass a drug screening and criminal background check.

The Academy selection process is very competitive and is based on a point system that includes 100 points for the written exam and 100 points for fitness evaluation. Ten additional points each can be awarded for military experience, a fire science degree from any accredited college or being a certified NREMT-Basic or Paramedic. Fire Department Explorers can earn an additional 5 points.

Applicants accepted to the academy will require tuition and fees for Arizona Residents of $2,990. The fee for the background check is $49.50 and a $50 fee for the written examination. Recruits will be responsible for the cost and scheduling of their physical examination from a physician of their choice.

Firefighter / Paramedic Jon Irula is Mohave Community Colleges' Fire Academy Coordinator. Jon covers over 150 Job Performance Skills or JPR's that candidates must show competency in before graduating and accepting their state certificate.

Fireboat

Before They Can Launch

First the crew must load aboard and drive the engine to Contact Point
[one exit south of Mulberry, to the right] ...

... down the ramp ...

Before reaching...

Engine 5, as well as the next closest unit would be dispatched to this 1,000 lb. all-metal watercraft. From leaving the station in their engine, to reaching the boat, lowering, and launching takes approximately 5-8 Minutes. The boat travels at approximately 35 MPH.

Minimum crew needed for major emergencies:

1 Man Driving

1 Man dedicated to command

2 Men to assist with medical

Each station is currently only running 3-man teams – so multiple engines may be dispatched to the Fireboat for manpower. A delay caused by the synchronization of both Engines arriving at Contact Point and on the boat ready to launch.

Front of boat dropped into the water.

This boat, which Lake Havasu City Fire Department has owned and operated for the past 6 years, has a winched drop down front, used for water rescues (C Spine Injuries), floating a backboard under the patient, they can then easily slide them onto the deck.

Being able to walk the patient off the deck is much safer than lifting them over the side of the boat.

On The Fireboat

The boats are equipped with everything a fire engine would have, except the heat monitor and drug-box, which is brought onboard at the time they disembark.

Junk Box & Clipboards (for reports) →

← **Medical Storage**
Multiple medical aid kits
for handling multiple patients.

Fire Pumps

The boat is equipped with two (2) 500 Gallon-Per-Minute Fire Pumps (one for each side).

←Master On/Off, under the Fire Pump
(shown above)

The big pipe going down goes into the lake – it pumps water from there to the various fire pumps.

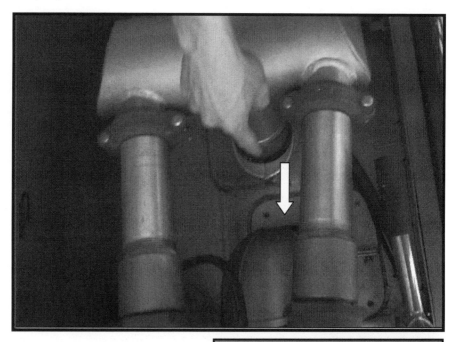

The 500 gallon per minute pressure can cause the boat to turn. Pump Operators must communicate with the boat operator, via these wireless headphones.

Class-B Foam

The boat has a built in foam tank under the deck for fuel tank involved boat fires.

Each side also has connections for a standard fire hose for close brushfires.

Grappling Hook

This grappling hook, attached to the fireboat, is used to keep a burning boat a set distance from the fireboat, as well as keeps it from pushing away from them as they fight the fire.

Floating Backboard

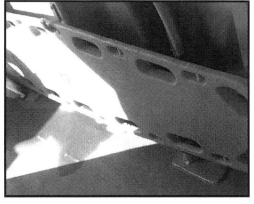

When there's no one behind the controls...

... it's time to put the Fire Boat away.

The boat is lifted out of the water once at the dock.

- 3 Coast Guard Approved Boat Captains
- Lake Rescue Capabilities for Entire Lake from Parker Dam to I-40
- Firefighting Capabilities along the Entire Shoreline of Lake Havasu

HAZMAT

Station #2 houses the HAZMAT truck and trailer, overseen by "A-SHIFT".

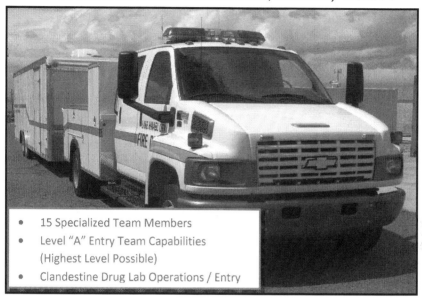

- 15 Specialized Team Members
- Level "A" Entry Team Capabilities (Highest Level Possible)
- Clandestine Drug Lab Operations / Entry

Due to the increase in the perceived threat of terrorism in the early 21st century after the September 11, 2001 attacks, funding for greater HAZMAT-handling capabilities were increased throughout the United States, recognizing that flammable, poisonous, explosive, or radioactive substances in particular could be used for terrorist attacks. (Extracted from Wikipedia)

HAZMAT Truck

Lighting

Cribbing

Chains

Grounding Wires

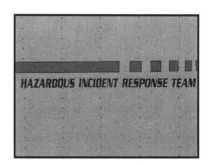

Remote Communication System & Wiring in case wireless radio communication is not possible.

Caution Tape, "Plug & Dyke" which turns into a rubber compound when mixed with liquid.

4 air-tank refills (two per side of the truck), Pony Bottles (5 min. "spare air"), wood plugs for plugging up 55 gal. barrel drums and keep them from leaking, "Over Barrels" can hold a 55 gallon barrel inside for containing/sealing the hazard.

LHCFD does not transport hazardous materials; a third-party company would assist.

HAZMAT Trailer

Stretchable decontaminating tunneling which can spray those traveling within it.

Pre-fitted HAZMAT Gear (belts, hoods, overalls, over boots, earplugs, gloves, etc.) for each team member to allow for quicker response.

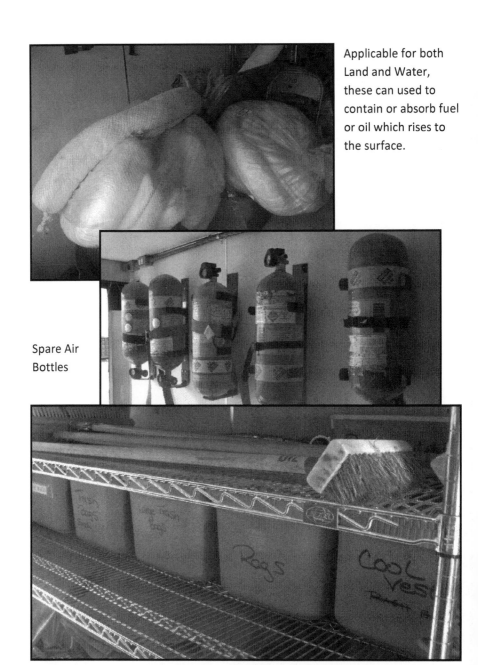

Applicable for both Land and Water, these can used to contain or absorb fuel or oil which rises to the surface.

Spare Air Bottles

Trash Bags, Body Bags, Rags, Vests and brushes for scrub-downs.

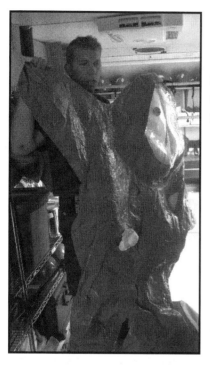

Engineer Justin Bacon holds up a flash suit as he explains, "It's Insulated, chemical proof – made to resist fire".

Gloves

Baby Powder

Bars of Soap

Extra Pairs of Sandals for changing into after a clean-up.

Extra Radios and Fire/Rescue Helmets similar to Firefighter helmets without the bill, flame retardant flaps, and face shield.

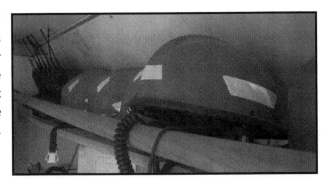

Chemistry Kit and Flow Chart to test for hazardous solids & liquids such as arsenic, anthrax, menthol, round-up, etc. – LHCFD now has a "HAZMAT ID" computer which will quickly identify the material.

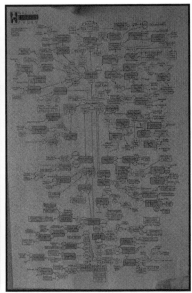

RESCUE 42

The number "42" given by the Station it's housed at, Station 4, and the 2 because it's the second unit at that station.

Purchased with a grant, this vehicle is like an "ultimate construction vehicle". Let me share with you some of the capabilities and items it offers.

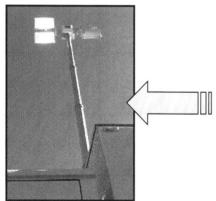

This light is as bright as lights on the football field.

Remote operated boom light on top. Buttons light up for available options.

Cordless Power Tools
Basic Hand Tools – Sawzaw,
Skill Saws, drills

Cutting Torch, Chop Saw

Confined Spaces
Jacketed Airline &
communications line

Super-Size Jack Hammer

Compressor/Stokes Basket
For Nail Guns

Air Packs

Medical Equipment
Setup like Engines.

Gas Powered Tools
Chainsaw, Gas Cans, Concrete Circular Saw,
Boring Drill, 2x 2000 Watt Generators

Stabilization Struts & Chains

Ladders / 2x4 Lumber / Backboards

← **Swift Water Rescue Packs**

ARIZONA VORTEXT MULTIPOD
Designed by a TRT Firemen here in
Arizona, provides a portable base
for rescuers to rappel.

Forcible Entry Tools – Shovels, Axes, Pry Bars, Sledge Hammers

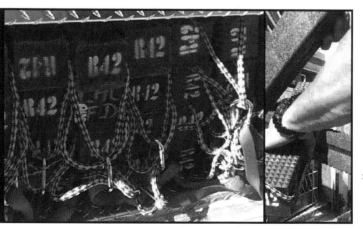

Cribbing - Stackable blocks and wedges that can be used for vehicle stabilization.

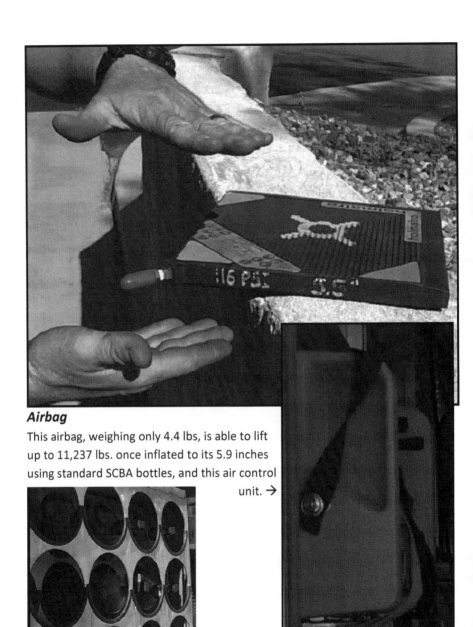

Airbag

This airbag, weighing only 4.4 lbs, is able to lift up to 11,237 lbs. once inflated to its 5.9 inches using standard SCBA bottles, and this air control unit. →

Extra
SCBA
Bottles

Remote Air-Control Unit

This unit can be used with the Remote Air & Communications equipment to control air for rescuers, run tools, or both. Swap out one bottle while running off the other.

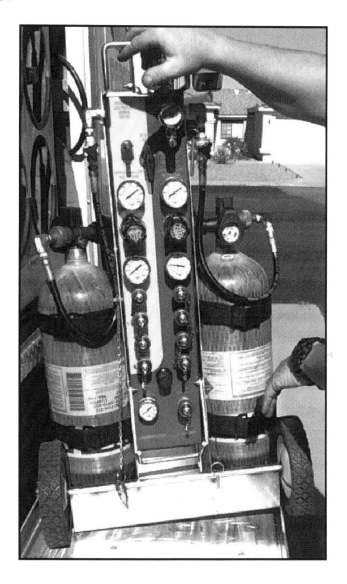

12,000 LBS. Winch

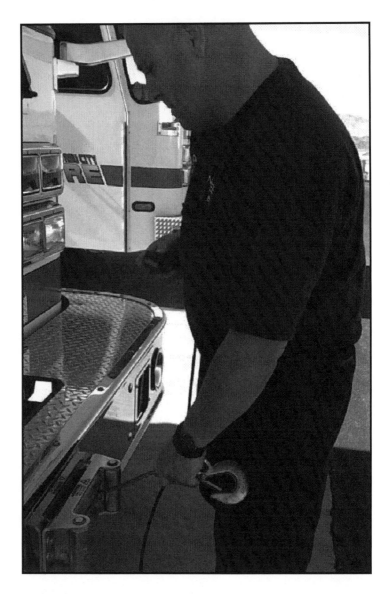

Thanks to Engineer Mike Connelly for sharing Rescue 42 with us.

Aircraft Rescue Fire Fighting Apparatus (ARFF)
1999 Titan E1

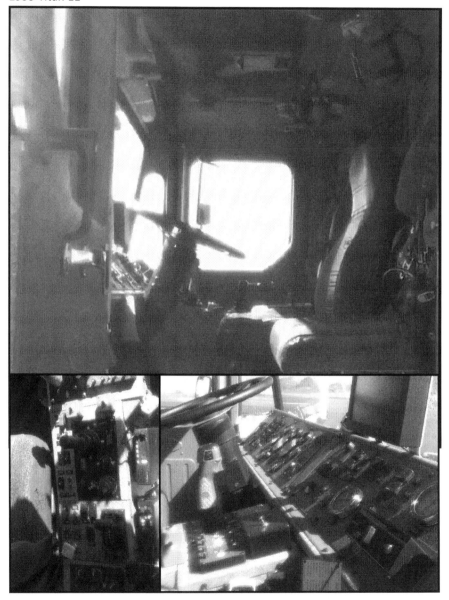

Joystick-like control the "bumper turret" and "roof turret", seen on the next page.

Bumper Turret   Roof Turret

The Turrets' spray Water, Foam, and Purple-K (also known as PKP, a dry-chemical fire suppression agent used in dry powder fire extinguishers, most effective in fighting Class B flammable liquid fires).

INTERESTING FACT!   ARFF can hold 1600 gallons of water, and 223 gallons of foam.

Why are the tires so big?

Boasting big tires and four-wheel drive, the ARFF is designed for off-road purposes, because best scenario - an airplane remains on the landing strip; otherwise they may end up on the dirt or out in the hills.

Inch and three-quarter hand-line (shown far left) deploys water. A large array of extrication tools to cut into the side of an aircraft, including a circular saw (shown far right). Hazmat containment equipment.

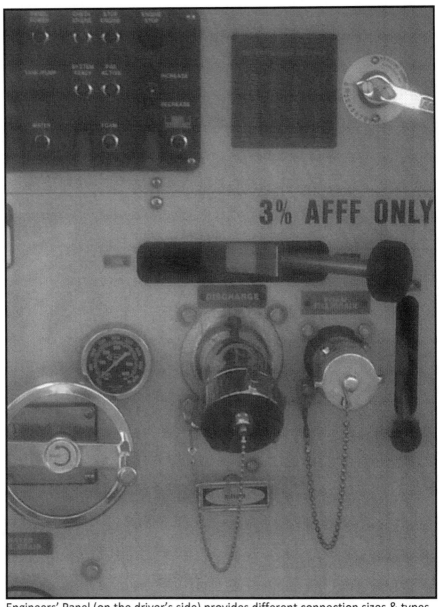

Engineers' Panel (on the driver's side) provides different connection sizes & types of discharge. Foam concentration is also controlled at this panel.

The roof of the apparatus is where a generator is stored, ladders, and a "piercing nozzle" (allows firefighters to spear the aircraft & spray through holes in the end).

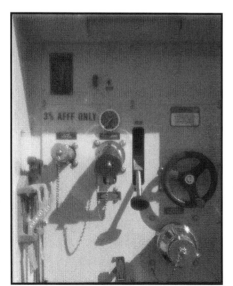

← Engineer Panel #2 (Passenger Side)

Hallotron System – Powder Suppression System, which allows minimal damage to the inside of the aircraft.

Booster Line – deploys water and foam, controlled by
either of the Engineer Panels, or inside of the AARF vehicle.

The bottom side contains a sprinkler system that once activated from within the cab, will spray a blanket of foam to keep the apparatus zone safe.

A spray system is also located just above the windshield to allow the apparatus to get in as close as possible to perform a rescue and still keep the vehicle cool.

Emergency Management "Homeland Security"

As part of the emergency response system in Lake Havasu City, the Fire Department manages the disaster preparedness program. This program has been designed to manage emergency response to the many types of disasters that can occur within the city.

Some disaster prepared issues that affect Lake Havasu City are:

- Flash Flooding
- Major Fire
- High Winds
- Extreme Heat
- Hazardous Materials Issues
- Domestic Terrorism
- Civic Disturbance
- Extended Power Outage
- Earthquake (Moderate Issue)

Emergency Management Training:

- City officials periodically attend the National Emergency Training Center in Emmitsberg, Maryland.
- Lake Havasu City participates in at least one disaster exercise each year at the local or state level.
- A community of people from all areas of disaster response meets quarterly to discuss issues and evaluate the City Emergency Operations Plan (EOP).

Lake Havasu Emergency Management Accomplishments and Memberships:

- Received a FEMA award for the full-scale exercise hosted in 2000.
- Was showcase city at the National League of Cities Convention in 2004.
- Nationally recognized by FEMA for the City's Y2K plan in 1999.
- Member of Arizona Emergency Services Association.
- Member of the Mohave County Local Emergency Planning Committee.
- Received $429,392 in grants for equipment and training in the 2004/2005 fiscal year.
- Assisted the Bureau of Reclamation planning efforts for catastrophic dam failure along the Colorado River.

Other LHCFD Service Offerings

"Fire Safety" in Home/Business/Assembly – lessons in fire prevention, fire extinguishers, fire escape plans, disaster preparedness, etc.

"Fire Extinguisher Class" – a program specifically designed for civic, business or company groups. This is a simulated fire training class on the proper use of fire extinguishers with a state of the art prop.

"Safety Lessons for Scouts" – various programs to meet the requirements of specific badges.

"Fire Safety for Senior Citizens" – a program specifically designed for the safety of senior citizens.

"Juvenile Fire Setter Program" – classes for children who have started fires or have an interest in fire. The children are taught about burn injuries and safe behaviors. We also instruct the parents how to keep their home safe from such activity. (This program is taught one on one, not in a group setting).

"T.Y.K.S. Child Safety" – Teaching parents/guardians how to be more aware of hazards in the home that could lead to accidents involving children.

"Baby Sitting Classes"

Call Administrative Assistant, Kathy, at 928-855-3609 with questions regarding any of these programs.

Ref: http://www.lhcaz.gov/fire/publicEducation.html

Firefighters Association

MISSION STATEMENT
The Lake Havasu Professional Firefighters Association through a strong commitment to the Labor-Management Process will strive to safeguard and improve the safety and welfare of all members and improve our community and department through positive interaction with our citizens, elected officials and administrators.

Tim Maple is the current present of the Lake Havasu City Professional Firefighters Association (LHCPFFA).

Events that the Association hosts:

* Toy Drive
*Child Education
* School Demonstrations
* Donny D Memorial Fund
* Pink Shirt Breast Cancer Awareness
* Retired Firefighters

LHCFD / AMR Cooperative

As of Monday, July 9, 2012 at 7 AM, River Medical Inc. (a division of AMR) and Lake Havasu City Fire Department (LHCFD) officially began a joint staffing program which supports a Public-Private Partnership (P3) between the two agencies.

The arrangement calls for River Medical to supply two ambulances with an EMT driver for each unit, and LHCFD to provide a Paramedic for each unit, as well as accommodations at Station #1 on Acoma Blvd., and Station #2 on Kiowa (pictured below).

In addition to these two units, River Medical will continue to operate four additional [non LHCFD marked] units with the goal of "reducing response times to major incidents while reducing the number of large firefighting apparatus responding to minor incidents throughout the community." says Fire Chief Dennis Mueller.

$300,000 annual gain in the City's General Fund are being paid by River Medical for use of the Fire Stations and its Paramedics.

Firefighter-EMT's are restricted from performing Firefighter capabilities while assigned to the ambulance, even in a fire.

Currently LHC Dispatch alerts the call, while RMI overhears and controls responders.

RIVER MEDICAL INC.

a division of American Medical Response

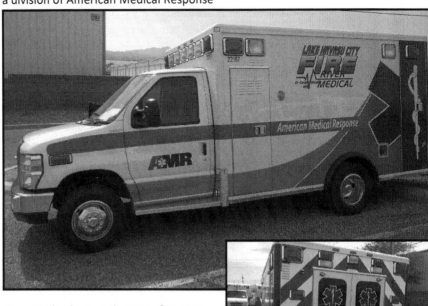

River Medical Inc., a division of American Medical Response (AMR) - has partnered with the Lake Havasu City Fire Dept. to joint-staff two (2) dedicated ambulances to cover "A Level" calls received by 9-1-1.

IV Bags, Tubing, and C-Spine

Gauze, Bandages, Trauma Dressings

Suction Equipment – for clearing obstructions such as vomit, etc. in airways.

(Left) **Emergency Blankets**   (Right) **Basic Ice Packs**

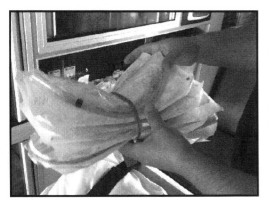

ET Tubes – For when a patient is unable to protect their own airway, the Paramedics can use this to establish an airway and breathe for the patient.

IV Catheters (Intravenous). 22 gauge (smallest) to 16 gauge (largest)

Mobile Gear
Everything inside the Ambulances, is also ready to go mobile from the inside or outside the ambulance.

Sharps Container
Used to dispose of dirty needles, and prevent the spread of deadly viruses to other patients or medical staff.

Glove Compartment

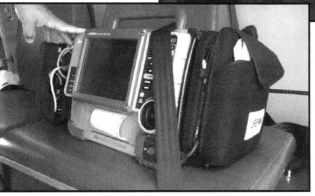

← **LIFEPAK AED:**
Defibrillator
Blood Pressure
CO2 Monitoring

This highly specialized monitoring equipment has the capability to transmit EKG's directly to the ER or the cell phones or computers of Cardiologists, so if necessary, the patient can be taken directly to the Cardiac Cath Lab for expedited treatment of certain types of heart attacks.

DID YOU KNOW? It takes three (3) batteries to power each ambulance.

Much like the Police Vehicles and Fire Engines, today's Medics and Ambulances are also trained and equipped with Toughbooks - also known as **MDT (Mobile Data Terminal)**. The screen swivels, and are touch screen.

This screen swiveling and touch screen capable device provides Electronic Charting (vs. Paper Charting), which allows the information to come from the Dispatch CAD System right into the computer. No lost Paperwork, Delay in Paperwork, straight to the Billing Office to be handled electronically.

The Front Cab - The EMT will drive the ambulance, while the Paramedic sits in the passenger's seat doing mapping, listen to Fire Departments' traffic, and communicating with RMI dispatch.

Utilized on major holidays and large lake events, the **River Medical Safety Boat** is operated at no-cost to the community, providing additional coverage on such a large coverage area.

River Medical Inc. – Inside Dispatch

One of Three RMI Dispatch Workstations

Out of Lake Havasu's "STATION 19", River Medical Inc. dispatches for Mohave County, La Paz County, up to Yavapai County Border, Kingman, Blyth, and more.

9-1-1 call information is given to RMI dispatch from LHC Fire Dispatch via phone.

Lake Havasu City runs approximately 4-7 ambulances within city limits at any given time.

"Charlie" and "Delta" level calls are more severe, while "Alpha" and "Bravo" are less severe.

Interested in becoming a Medical Dispatcher?
"You must first receive your "Emergency Medical Dispatch License" to learn protocol, and be dedicated" – John D., Dispatch Supervisor

Air Methods Corporation

Formally Native Air/ Omni Flight, this newly bought-out partnership (August of 2011) by Air Methods Corporation has provided great training, and newly purchased equipment such as a new 2011 ASB350+ aka "A-Star" helicopter, based here at Havasu Regional Medical Center.

Capable of providing the same level of service that you would receive in an Intensive Care Unit (ICU) – let's go in for a closer look...

Slide-Out Gurney allows the patient to be transferred by the Fire Department by their Backboard.

Backseat Pouches
The back of the pilots' seat offers Flight Medics small airway devices, bandages, and gloves.

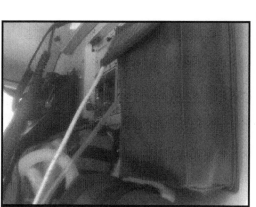

Behind the seats acting as a headrest, are IV Supplies and other supplies such as a valve mask.

IV Kits aka "Drug Bags" (above) are kept under the seats and contain all the medications necessary to allow the flight medical crew to do their job effectively.

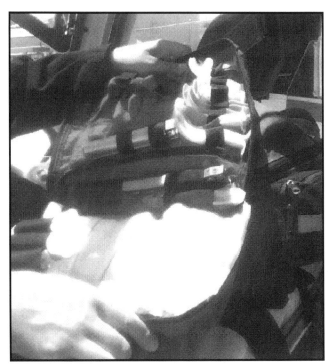

Intubation tools as shown to the left, allow the medical team to put a tube into a subjects throat if they are unable to breath for themselves.

Part of the **Trauma Bag** (in background) contains Splints, another IV Kit, bandages, and dressings.

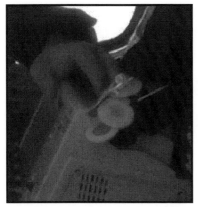

← **Heart Monitor** – Allows the medical team to pace a person's heart, when beating abnormally. They can shock or defibrillate the heart for someone in cardiac arrest. A 12-Lead EKG allows 12 different views of the heart.

IV Pumps →
Able to run up to 6 drip medications that may require specific amounts at one time, able to dispense micro-grams a minute. This unit is now discontinued.

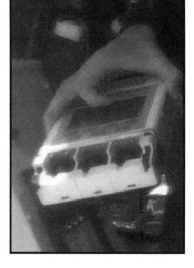

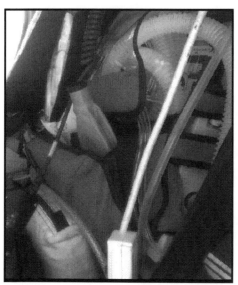

← **Ventilator**
Equivalent to any standard ICU equipment in America, medics are able to breath for patients. This tool has saved many from having to be intubated.

← Liquid Oxygen Tank

This new helicopter provides enough Liquid Oxygen to run several flights, or handle multiple patients at once.

Located in the rear compartment on the pilots' side - paperwork, extra set of headphones, and the Liquid Oxygen Tank displayed at the top of this page.

Pediatric Board, PediMate (Child size restraint system that attaches to existing), Splints, First Aid Kit, and portable pacemaker.

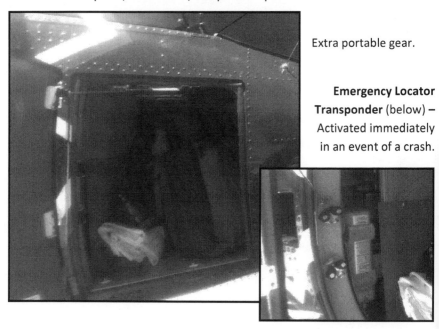

Extra portable gear.

Emergency Locator Transponder (below) – Activated immediately in an event of a crash.

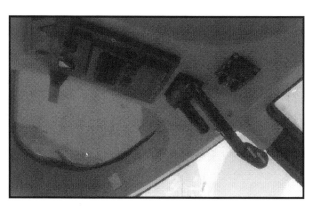

Rotor Break (longer) will stop the blades from rotating.

Fuel Cutoff (shorter) shuts off all fuel to the aircraft.

Engine Start/Run switches.

NVG Compatible Lighting Filtered or Green Light, allowing the medical team to see while using Night Vision Goggles.

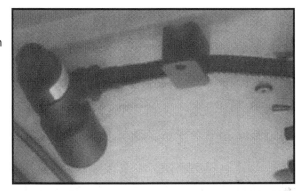

The pilots' control displays are also filtered as to not interfere with the medical team while using Night Vision.

Pilots' Controls (above)

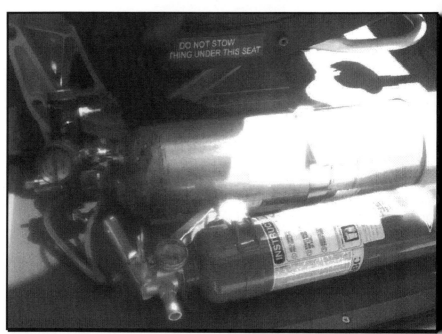

Fire Extinguisher and Portable Oxygen Tank – already on the gurney, this one may be used when transporting a patient out of the ER and onto the aircraft.

Testimonials for Emergency Personnel

The follow are just some of the praise that we've seen going over the internet for our local Emergency Service Personnel.

Danette Shoop – *"Just wanted to say that you are all very much appreciated. I have needed you many times and you have always been there. You do a great job."*

"Thank you to all Firefighters and police officers…" **Mike Mascari** says *"… for saving us from a lot of sorrow and pain. I raise my glass and toast to you and your families for your lives!!! Also to the fallen members we all love you and miss you, and will always have a home in our hearts for you and your families!!!!"*

*"In January [2012] we had a small house fire at 3:30 AM. The Lake Havasu City Fire Department arrived before I got off the phone with 9-1-1! They were here within three minutes of my call…"*says **Stephanie Contreras** *"… it was freezing outside and one of the firemen gave me his jacket to stay warm. They took care of the fire and took the broken drywall out. Thank you LHC FD!"*

"Thank you to all of our emergency response teams. To the Police for trying to keep our streets safe, to the Fire Department for everything you do, to the EMTs, for search and rescue teams. All of you deserve many thanks for being hero's to each of the families you have helped, for being role models for the children in our town and for being selfless in all you do."
- Amanda Lain

Misty Halliday – *"My son Daniel was blessed by the love and support that our local PD and Firefighters showed as they lined the walls of his funeral service and my family and friends were touched and their presence! Among the sorrow of the day they brought a soft touch to the hearts and I feel as though I never properly said "Thank You!" – so from the entire family we give thanks and support to your fight to keeping us safe!"* **(The Halliday Family)**

"Thank you for your service/dedication! My 9 year old daughter loves to go to the fire station and learn and she loves how nice they are, she tells me every time how much she respects them!!!" **– Amber Mckinney**

Nissa Harris – *"My husband's life was SAVED last Thursday due to the fast response and care given by the personnel at Station #3. Wonderful crew, they are incredible!"*

"When I was 8 months along with my son, I was involved in a bad car accident. Thanks to a fast response from Fire Station #2 and EMT's, I was safely removed from the vehicle and transported to the hospital in time to have a healthy baby boy, who just turned 2.

Thank you to all men and women who serve with the Police, Fire, and River Medical Inc (independent ambulance service) for all you do and all that you put on the line to save the rest of us when we need it most."
- **Paige Laven**

Jane Kendall – *"Our Police Department does an outstanding job in every aspect. Our Fire Department and Medics/EMT crews are awesome. Don't forget the first responders on the phone with you till help gets there; our 9-1-1 Dispatchers who are all EMD trained to help you while help is on the way. Thank you for everything you do."*

"It's two or three o'clock in the morning on any given morning there is a fire; or a medical emergency; or someone hears a prowler - The Lake Havasu City Fire and Police respond, not because they get paid to, but because they're dedicated to their jobs. They take pride in what they do and this is why I would consider our first responders the best there is. Let's not forget our 9-1-1 Dispatchers as this is where it all starts - their calming voice saves lives before the responders arrive. Thank you All."
- Ken Lowry

"All of the area emergency responders here deserve a standing ovation! Thanks to each and every one of you! **– Nannette Billings**

Patrisha S. Endelman

WE have awesome firefighters. These men and women put their lives on the line for us EVERYDAY...i know this from personal experience and i thank them!!!!

Friday at 5:19pm ·

Donna McDaniel Francis

To our son, Brian - Firefighter/Paramedic and all of his fellow Firefighters/Paramedic family.... We are so proud of you and send our love and prayers to all! :) ♥

Like · Comment · Friday at 4:05pm ·

 Donna McDaniel Francis and 6 others like this.

Lori Scott

THANK YOU ALL FIREFIGHTERS!

Like · Comment · Friday at 11:20am ·

10 people like this.

Dorothy Garrett I am so proud of both my sons, both firefighters and all the guys and gals they work with.

Friday at 10:27pm · Unlike · 1

About Havasu Scanner Feed

HSF Mission Statement

The Mission of Havasu Scanner Feed is to educate you on the operational methods of our emergency services and personnel, and interact with you in ways which increase your safety and awareness.

In The News

The following is an authorized REPRINT from Today's News Herald: HavasuNews.com

Robert Starkey, 30, founder of Havasu Scanner Feed

Robert Starkey had no idea that the Facebook page he created airing behind-the-scenes audio of Lake Havasu City's police and fire departments responding to emergencies would become so popular.

But it has.

Around 9:30 a.m. Saturday, the 30-year-old pulled up Havasu Scanner Feed and even though the scanner was quiet, the site still showed that 21 people were listening.

When the page went live two months ago, one person had "liked" it. As of 1:25 p.m. Saturday, that number reached 3,751. On average, 63 new people a day have been "liking" the page since it began.

"This monster will take off on its' own," he said.

Starkey basically just hooked up a police and fire scanner — available in retail stores — and tuned into Lake Havasu City's frequencies so that emergency dispatch calls feed into the webpage 24 hours a day, seven days a week. Anyone older than 18 years old can "like" the page and listen to the city's police and fire departments being dispatched to emergencies within the city.

But that audio access also includes being able to hear citizens' names needing an emergency response and their addresses.

Enthusiasts of Havasu Scanner Feed have started volunteering their time by posting what they hear over the scanner onto the webpage, but anyone can post what they hear. Readers can also get the alerts on their cell phones.

However, one of the page's rules is to not post names or exact addresses, and the webpage's administrative team is diligent to enforce the rules by monitoring posts constantly. For now, Starkey and the volunteers just monitor and post whenever they can. There is no schedule or shifts, but he admitted that if the page continues to grow in popularity, he may need some help.

"I can't be doing this 24 hours a day, seven days a week," said the full-time disc jockey. "It's having an inside scoop. It's knowing what's happening before the newspaper can get to it."

Posts like: "vehicle in building Dollar General. On Maricopa" posted around 12:08 p.m. Saturday. Earlier that day, around 5 a.m., someone posted: "#medical# #police# Injo woman is reporting sick and suicidal wants psychiatric help." And even in the earlier morning hours, someone had posted: "MEDICAL# 50-year-old male fell in driveway and is bleeding from nose and mouth, Keywester and Venturer Ln."

Starkey said he used to listen to scanners when he was younger and stumbled across a similar site for Lake Havasu City that he decided to help improve. Eventually, he took over the information, he said.

He said he started the webpage without first consulting with the city's police and fire departments, but he said the public's constant access to the emergency personnel calls makes it more aware of what's happening in the community.

And police and fire department officials agree, but still have concerns that the site might draw the curious out to scenes of accidents and crimes and hinder emergency personnel's work.

"We support the public having as much knowledge and information about what their police department is doing that goes along with Chief Doyle's philosophy of running a transparent department," said Lake Havasu City Police Department Spokesman Sgt. Joe Harrold. "(But) let the police department, who is trained to handle these situations, let them do their job."

Harrold also said he was concerned about wrong information being posted that could potentially cause harm to residents.

Someone posted on the site at 10:59 a.m July 21 that there was a deceased grandmother in the 4000 block of Northstar Drive, but it was the grandmother who had called police and reported that it was her grandson who was possibly deceased.

"Anybody can go out and buy a scanner and plug into our frequencies and listen," Harrold said. "There are no issues there. We see this as a great tool. It could certainly benefit the community, but at the same time, we want folks to use it as it was meant, a receipt of information. An informed public is a safer public." Lake Havasu City Fire Department Capt. Tony Rivello called the site "amazing."

"By having that information in front of their face, they are actually able to see what's going on in the community," Rivello said. "So many people really have no idea of the things that are occurring right in their own backyard. I was thoroughly impressed with how fast his subscribers grew on his page."

Rivello echoed Harrold's concerns over residents arriving on scene to see what's happening. He said users should treat the webpage as a "news feed."

He also said he had concerns about residents' privacy, but said the webpage's administration team has "some very good ground rules" for its volunteers who post information.

"We would not (want to) compromise anybody's privacy or expose anybody's identity that they may not get otherwise," he said. "It's a little more serious business and it's an opportunity for people in the community to see what's happening in a news feed relationships to police and fire."

But both Harrold and Rivello said the release of information could sway residents in the opposite direction of rubberneckers by helping them to steer clear of crime and accident scenes.

But Starkey and other volunteers said they can only see the webpage helping the community. Several posts on the page ask for the crisis hotline number and one poster suggested forming a neighborhood watch group.

Starkey said they don't post certain alerts and noticed teens and children were ringing doorbells and running away or calling 9-1-1 and hanging up just to see it post to the webpage, which led to their ban.

"Most of the people that go on there say we had no idea what's going on in the town," said 29-year-old Sarah Berger, one of the volunteers. "I was amazed at all the stuff that does happen."

A LOT HAS IMPROVED SINCE THE ABOVE ARTICLE RAN...

HSF General Guidelines

- Members should be 18+ years of age.
- Do not rush to anything you may hear via our Live Feed.
- Do not look-up, contact, or harass any person whose name may be transmitted via airwaves or in print.
- Do not record or re-transmit license plate numbers, driver's licenses or names of parties investigated by the police department.

What HSF does not post

- We do not post physical addresses, only block numbers and the street name. (example: 1400 block of John Street)
- We do not post exact ages. All ages are rounded down.
- For officer safety, we may reserve posting until officer is on scene.
- We do not post Unit Numbers of the patrol units or fire department engine numbers.
- We do not post stakeout or DUI checkpoint information
- We do not post Priority 3 Calls (doorbell ditch, barking dogs) and rarely 9-1-1 hang-ups.
- We do not post assisted living/nursing home calls:

Havasu Nursing Home	3576 Kearsage Drive
Casa Grande Assisted Living	3801 Buena Vista Drive
Haven House Assisted Living	1791 Cliffrose Drive
House on the Riviera	190 Riviera Drive
Lake Hills Inn	2781 Osborn Drive
Jasmine House	3076 Shoshone Drive
Lake View Terrace	320 N. Lake Havasu Avenue
Prestige Assisted Living	1221 Claremont Drive
	90 S. Smoketree Avenue
Serenity Assisted Living	3677 Blue Colt Drive
Sun Haven Assisted Living	2731 S. Jamaica Blvd
Beckett House	Multiple Addresses on Cashemere

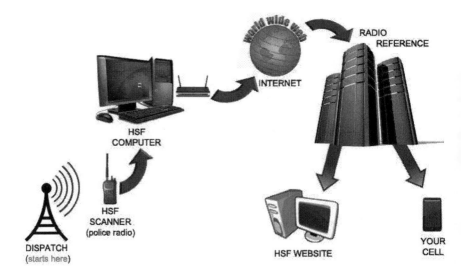

Live Feed

We provide a live streaming audio feed of the transmissions received from Lake Havasu City Dispatch. We welcome our community to listen to it, instead of arriving on scene of an incident. You are more likely to know what's going on by following our website – http://www.HavasuScannerFeed.com

Printed Feed

Our team of community volunteers post calls dispatched by Lake Havasu City's Police & Fire Dispatch Center located inside of the Police Station. These posts are then received via Facebook, our Website, Twitter, or Cellular SMS.

Each call is identified not by the service provider, but by the type of call. **#POLICE#   #FIRE#   #MEDICAL#**   followed by nature of the call (i.e. "ill female"), then the block number and street. Any additional details that are important for the community to know, will follow.

> **RE: Missing Person Posts** Per Lake Havasu City Police Department, we are to post "Missing Persons" calls as we know: (a) Child/Adults Name; (b) Exact Age (this is the only time we will post a child's exact age); (c) Clothing Description; (d) Last Seen – Time, Location, and Direction of Travel.

Facebook Friend Stream

"LIKE" our Facebook Page and our posts will display on your Friend Feed Stream.

Share On Facebook

"SHARE" allows you to voice your opinion on a call, without interrupting the flow of our service. The post and your comment go on your profile wall instead of ours.

Online Videos

LHCPD

LHCFD

Right from our website our visitors can watch "A message from the LHCPD Chief", "Message from Fire Station #2 Captain Tony Rivello".

Other Bonus Videos (used to create this book) are available from our Website at http://www.HavasuScannerFeed.com and include the following:

Segment 1 – FD: Virtual Firehouse Tour

Segment 2 – FD: Mapping (Paper and Computer Aided)

Segment 3 – FD: Inside The Fire Engine

Segment 4 – FD: The Fireboat

Segment 5 – FD: Rescue 42

Segment 6 – FD: Airport Rescue (ARFF)

Segment 7 – RMI: Inside The Ambulance

Segment 8 – RMI: Inside The Dispatch Center

Segment 9 – PD/FD: Inside The Dispatch

Segment 10 – PD: Mobile Crime Scene Van

Segment 11 – PD: The Motorcycle

Segment 12 – PD: The Sergeant's Vehicle

Segment 13 – PD: Indoor Firing Range

Segment 14 – AM: Helicopter Tour

Segment 15 – Desert Hills FD

Fundraising

"Copy for D.A.R.E."

Havasu Scanner Feed collected over $600 from local businesses, in our first year of being established, to benefit the LHC PD for our local D.A.R.E. Program.

"10-4 For Kids Fire Safety"

In our second fundraiser in our first year of existence, Havasu Scanner Feed collected over $300 in funds for the LHCPFFA's "Children's In-Classroom Education".

Suicide Awareness & Intervention

Havasu Scanner Feed was the first to organize a free community event to openly discuss the topic of Suicide. We reviewed Stats with Sgt. Joe Harold, Dr. Lumpkin, as well as opened free booth space for Interagency, Southwest Behavioral Health, AZ Department of Health Services, HART, Heartbeat, Women with Willpower, and received public recognition front page from Today's News Harold.

Ref:http://www.havasunews.com/articles/2012/03/03/news/doc4ebf3fe4c33fd180913318.txt

Police/Fire Frequencies

Scanner enthusiasts looking to follow the action from their own Digital Scanners will need to be able to receive from LHC Dispatch's Motorola Type II Smartnet system. You'll start to hear the action as soon as you program in the following 800 Frequencies:

855-23750	857.48750
855-96250	858.23750
856.23750	859.26250
856.43750	860.43750
857.23750	860.96250

(The above was last updated on Oct 22, 2011 – Thanks Gilligan, "Flano", Eric, Dan, and "Thunderbolt")

Fire & EMS Talkgroups

DEC	HEX	Alpha Tag	Description
176	00b	LH – EMS	EMS Dispatch
3216	0c9	LHFD – Z2Ch8	Zone 2, Channel 8
3280	0cd	LHFD F1 Disp	Fire 1 – Dispatch
3312	0cf	LHFD F2	Fire 2
3344	0d1	LHFD F3	Fire 3 – Fire Ground
3376	0d3	LHFD F4	Fire 4
3408	0d5	LHFD F5	Fire 5
3504	0db	LHFD INSPECT	Fire Inspectors
3536	0dd	LHFD ZbCH7	Zone B, Channel 7 (Training)

Police Talkgroups

DEC	HEX	Alpha Tag	Description
336	015	LHPD DISPTCH	Dispatch
368	017	LHPD INFO	Info
432	01b	LHPD Ch 4	Channel 4
464	01d	LHPD C2C	Channel 5 (Car-to-Car)
112	007	LHPD Ch 6	Channel 6
496	01f	LHPD Ch 9	Channel 9
528	021	LHPD Ch 15	Channel 15
560	023	LHPD SURVEIL	Surveillance

Ref: http://www.RadioReference.com/apps/db/?ctid=101

What the community is saying

Jessica Villarreal – *"Honestly, I have to say that HSF is basically the reason I get on Facebook, it's awesome that you can get on the computer and find out what's going on around town and you can give your feedback on what's happening. All I can say is you guys are doing an awesome job keep up the good work."*

"This is an outstanding site that keeps us informed minute by minute, and it seems there is something going on minute by minute. LHFD and LHPD do an exceptional job in this city. GOD bless all of you."

- Marsha Brothers

Christine Avis – *"Havasu Scanner Feed is great for getting information out about what is going on in our community and helps us feel safe whether out and about or in our homes. Every day before I leave my house I check in to HSF to see what is going on and what to avoid on my way out when I get home to see what might have occurred in my neighborhood while I was gone. Thank you Robert and all the awesome volunteers for doing what you can for our community to help us feel safe."* ☺

"I love the fact that even though I am out of town for a week, I can still see what's going on and stay updated. The volunteer staff is amazing at keeping up with everything; I look forward to opening my FB account and seeing what is going on, not to mention that it gives the public some insight into what our local men and women in uniform deal with on a day-to-day basis!"

- Justin Holland

Josh Neskahi - *"I absolutely love Havasu Scanner Feed! I am always kept up with what's going on in town. I always know what's going on, what streets to avoid if there is something big, and even the little things are interesting to know. Wanting to become an officer, this feed is all I look forward to during the day, night, school, work... all the time during the day! I love HSF and I hope it is kept up and continued, you guys are doing a fantastic job! Keep it up!"* :D

"We really enjoy the info put out on suspicious activities, accidents, fires, etc. We check frequently and feel that do to the info and description of an individual, we were able to call dispatch and let them know about the individual walking in our neighborhood and feel that the info we provided lead to the person being caught. Thank you HAVASU SCANNER FEED. We do feel safer because of your info you put out and that of those who help update it."
- Barbara McPherson

Susan Leifer – *"Love being fed by "The Feed". Bonus: When I can't sleep at night and there's nothing but infomercials on, I tune-in to Havasu Scanner Feed. (It's not illegal, immoral or fattening). Problem is, you want to wake everyone else up and let THEM know what's going on in the wee hours of the morning."*

Erin DiBona Leisz
Thank Dan Doyle and Lake Havasu for being appreciative of the Havasu Scanner Feed......hopefully all of us apart of it r doing it so we can be good for our community like myself.....n help the officers lower crime

"Thank you Chief Doyle and Chief Mueller!"
- Robert

Identifiable Logos

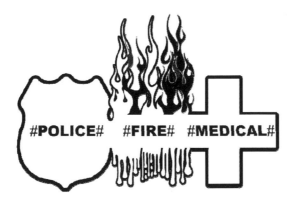

Arrest Reports

An Arrest Report is a legal document which provides a great detail of information on an arrest. A start to the paper trail for someone being entered into the justice system, this document is made available to the public from the Police Department, by request.

A volunteer member of the community operates the HSF "Arrest Reports" page. They review the report and transfer the arrest summary on the Facebook Page, via our Website, and made available to other outside news agencies and search engines. We also post "Cited & Released".

REPORTS

Another Identifiable Logo

Community Alerts

Also found on the Arrest Reports page, are "Community Alerts". These are notifications about crimes that are filed with the Police Department, in which a subject has not yet been arrested. These may commonly announce thefts, frauds, burglaries, graffiti, and other criminal damage.

Street Names

A

Acacia Lane
Acoma Blvd. N
Acoma Blvd. S
Acoma Blvd. W
Acoma Lane
Acoma Place
Admirals Bay
Adobe Drive
Agate Lane
Agave Drive
Agave Lane
Airport Road
Ajo Drive
Aladdin Drive
Alamo Lane
Albacore Drive
Albacore Lane
Albatross Lane
Alibi Drive
Allegheny Lane
Aloha Drive
Aloha Lane
Aloha Way
Alpaca Drive
Alpine Drive
Alpine Lane
Alta Lane
Alta Vista Drive
Amapola Drive
Ambas Drive
Ambassador Drive
Amberjack Bay E
Amberjack Bay W
Amberwood Avenue

Amberwood Bay N
Amberwood Bay S
Amberwood Circle
Amberwood Court
Amberwood Lane
Amberwood Place
Amigo Drive
Amigo Lane
Amigo Way
Anacapa Drive
Anacapa Place
Angelfish Drive
Angelfish Lane
Angler Drive
Angler Place
Anita Avenue
Anita Court
Ann Court
Antelope Drive
Apache Drive
Apache Maid Drive
Appian Drive
Appletree Drive
Applewood Drive
Applewood Place
Appaloosa Drive
Appaloosa Lane
Aqua Drive
Aquamarine Drive
Arabian Circle
Arabian Court
Arabian Drive
Arabian Lane
Arabian Plaza
Arapaho Drive
Arapaho Lane
Arcadia Drive

Arcadia Lane
Arizona HWY 95
Arizona Blvd.
Arizona Court
Arizona Lane
Arizona Place
Arizona Plaza
Armour Drive
Arnold Palmer Drive
Arrowhead Drive
Arrowwood Drive
Arroyo Drive
Arroyo Lane
Arthur Drive
Ascot Court
Ascot Drive
Ascot Way
Ash Drive
Aspen Drive
Atlantic Drive
Autumn Drive
Avalon Avenue
Avalon Bay
Avalon Circle
Avalon Court
Avalon Lane
Avalon Place
Avalon Plaza
Ave Laredo
Avenida Del Sol
Avenida Tierra Vista
Aviation Court
Aviation Drive
Avocado Lane
Aztec Drive
Azul Drive

B

Bahama Avenue
Bahia Hermosa
Bali Drive
Bamboo Court
Bamboo Drive
Bamboo Place
Barbara Drive
Barcelona Loop
Barite Drive
Baron Drive
Barranca Drive
Barranca Lane
Basin Drive
Baylor Drive
Bayou Lane
Bayshore Road
Baysinger Drive
Bayview Lane
Beachcomber Blvd.
Beachcomber Road
Beachview Drive
Beachview Lane
Bear Drive
Bear Way
Beavertail Drive
Beechwood Drive
Beefeater Drive
Beefeater Lane
Belair Lane
Bentley Blvd.
Bentley Court
Bermuda Avenue
Bermuda Court
Beverly Glen Court
Beverly Glen Drive
Beverly Glen Lane

Beverly Glen Place
Big Bass Cove
Big Chief Drive
Big Chief Way
Big Horn Drive
Bimini Lane
Birch Sq.
Birchett Lane
Birkdale Lane
Biscayne Lane
Bison Blvd.
Black Hill Bay
Black Hill Drive
Black Hill Place
Blackfoot Drive
Blackfoot Lane N
Blackfoot Lane S
Blackhawk Drive
Blue Canyon Road
Blue Colt Drive
Bluebird Drive
Bluecrest Drive
Bluecrest Lane
Bluecrest Place
Bluegill Drive
Bluegrass Bay
Bluegrass Circle
Bluegrass Court
Bluegrass Drive
Bluegrass Place
Bluegrass Plaza
Bluegrass Way
Bluewater Drive
Bluewater Lane
Boat Launch Road
Boeing Bay
Bombay Circle

Bombay Court
Bombay Drive
Bombay Lane
Bombay Place
Bombay Plaza N
Bombay Plaza S
Bonanza Drive
Bonanza Place
Bonita Lane
Bootleg Lane
Boros Lane
Bosun Lane
Boulder Drive
Bounty Lane
Bowie Drive
Bracero Lane
Brave Drive
Breakers Drive
Breakwater Drive
Breakwater Lane
Breakwater Place
Brewer Way
Briar Way
Briarcrest Drive
Brigs Lane
Brite Bay
Brite Drive
Broadwater Drive
Broadie Drive
Broken Arrow Drive
Brookside Drive
Broomrape Lane
Bryce Circle
Bryce Court
Bryce Drive
Bryce Lane
Bryce Place

Bryden Street
Buccaneer Lane
Buckboard Court
Buckboard Drive
Buckboard Lane
Buckboard Place
Buckboard Way
Buckingham Blvd.
Buckskin Drive
Buckwheat Lane
Buena Vista Avenue
Buena Vista Plaza
Bunker Drive
Buoy Drive
Buoy Lane
Burgundy Drive
Burgundy Lane
Burke Drive
Burke Lane
Burkemo Lane

C

Cabana Drive
Cactus Drive
Cactus Ridge Drive
Cactus Wren Drive
Cactus Wren Lane
Cadet Lane
Caesar Drive
Caesar Place
Cajon Lane
Caliente Drive
Caliente Lane
Calimesa Court
Calimesa Drive
Calle Del Oro
Calypso Drive

Camero Ctr.
Camero Drive
Camino Lane
Canal Lane
Candlewood Bay
Candlewood Drive
Candlewood Place
Candy Drive
Canterbury Road
Canyon Cove Drive
Canyon Drive
Canyon Oak Drive
Capri Blvd.
Caravan Drive
Caravelle Drive
Cardinal Drive
Caribbean Drive
Carlsbad Court
Carlsbad Drive
Carol Drive
Cascade Drive
Cascade Lane
Cashmere Drive
Casper Drive
Casper Lane
Castaway Drive
Castle Rock Bay Road
Catalina Drive
Catamaran Court
Catamaran Drive
Cataract Drive
Catchlaw Lane
Catfish Cove
Catherine Drive
Cattail Drive
Centers Avenue
Cerro Lane

Cessna Bay
Challenger Circle
Challenger Drive
Challenger Lane
Challenger Place
Chalon Drive
Chalon Lane
Chandler Circle
Chandler Drive
Chanute Drive
Chanute Place
Chaparral Circle
Chaparral Court
Chaparral Drive
Charing Cross Drive
Chelsea Circle
Chelsea Street
Chemehuevi Blvd
Chemehuevi Court
Chemehuevi Place
Chemehuevi Plaza
Chenoweth Road
Cheokee Lane
Cherry Tree Blvd.
Cherry Tree Place
Cherry Tree Way
Chesapeake Blvd.
Chesapeake Place
Cheyenne Lane
Chickasaw Drive
Chickasaw Lane
Chickasaw Plaza
Chinook Lane
Chip Drive
Chip Lane
Chipeta Lane
Chppewa Lane

Chiricahua Drive
Choate Lane
Choctaw Drive
Cholla Court
Cholla Drive
Cholla Plaza
Churchhill Bay
Churchill Drive
Cibola Lane
Cielo Drive
Cinnamon Bay
Cinnamon Drive
Cinnamon Lane
Circula de Hacienda
Circulo Hermosa
Cisco Drive N
Cisco Drive S
Citation Road
Citrus Lane
Civic Center Blvd.
Civic Center Lane
Claire Drive
Claremont Drive
Clarke Court
Clarke Drive
Clarke Place
Clarke Plaza
Clearwater Court
Clearwater Drive
Clearwater Lane
Cliffrose Drive
Cliffwood Court
Cliffwood Drive
Cliffwood Plaza
Clipper Lane
Cloverlawn Drive
Club House Drive

Coconino Drive
Coconut Grove Drive
College Drive
College Lane
Colt Drive
Columbia Court
Columbia Drive
Columbine Drive
Colville Drive
Comanche Lane
Combat Drive
Comet Drive
Commander Drive
Comstock Drive
Conestoga Drive
Constellation Drive
Constellation Lane
Continental Drive
Copper Drive
Coral Drive
Coral Reef Court
Coral Reef Drive
Coral Reef Lane
Coral Reef Place
Cork Lane
Corona Drive
Corotary Road
Corral Court
Corral Drive
Corsair Drive
Corte Cabrillo
Corte del Sol
Corte Estrella
Corte Fortuna
Corte Paloma
Corte Piedra
Corte Sienna

Corte Sur
Corte Teresa
Corte Tranquilla
Corvair Drive
Cosnina Drive
Cotati Drive
Cottonwood Drive
Cottonwood Plaza
Countryshire Avenue
Country HWY 233
Crater Circle
Crater Court
Crater Drive
Crater Way
Crazy Horse Drive
Crescent Drive
Crest Lane
Crestview Drive
Crestwind Drive
Cricket Lane
Crystal Avenue
Cumberland Bay
Cumberland Drive
Cup Drive
Cup Way
Curtis Drive
Cutlass Lane
Cutter Lane
Cypress Drive
Cypress Lane

D

Dafne Ln
Daniel Drive
Date Drive
Date Palm Drive
Date Row Drive

Date Row Lane
Dawn Drive
Dawn Way
Daytona Avenue
Daytona Lane
Daytona Loop
Daytona Place
Deacon Drive
Deepwater Drive
Deepwater Lane
Deer Run Circle
Deer Run Drive
Deer Run Lane Deer
Run Place
Deerpath Drive
Del Rey Drive
Del Rio Lane
Delta Drive
Demaret Drive
Desert Cove Drive
Desert Court
Desert Drive
Desert Garden Drive
Desert Glen Drive
Desert Hawk Drive
Desert Hills Estates
Desert Lake Drive
Desert Place
Desert Rose Drive
Desert Rose Lane
Desert Rose Place
Desert Sage Drive
Desert View Court
Desert View Drive
Diable Drive
Diamond Drive
Diane Drive

Dion Drive
Doeskin Drive
Doeskin Lane
Dogwood Drive
Dolphin Drive
Donna Drive
Donner Bay
Donner Circle
Donner Court
Donner Drive
Douglas Drive
Dover Avenue
Dover Court
Doyle Drive
Driftwood Drive
Drury Lane
Duel Drive
Duke Drive
Duke Lane
Dune Drive
Dune Lane
Dune Place

E

Eager Drive
Eagle Drive
Eagle Lane
Eagleton Lane
Eastwind Drive
Edgewater Blvd.
Edgewood Drive
El Camino Drive
El Camino Way
El Dorado Avenue N
El Dorado Avenue S
El Porto Lane
El Rey Lane

El Rio Drive
El Toro Drive
El Torro Drive
Elctra Bay
Emerald Drive
Empire Court
Empire Drive
Empress Court
Empress Drive
Empress Lane
Enduro Circle
Enduro Drive
Ensign Lane
Enterprise Drive
Erwin Lane
Estrella Drive
Everglades Drive

F

Fairchild Bay
Falcon Drive
Fan Palm Drive
Felicidad Circle
Felicidad Drive
Fern Lane
Fiesta Drive
Fiesta Plaza
Fiesta Way
Firefly Circle
Firefly Drive
Firestone Place
Fisherman Court
Fisherman Drive
Flagship Drive
Flamingo Lane
Flint Drive
Florence Drive

Flying Cloud Drive
Folzman Drive
Foothill Drive
Foothill Place
Foothills Pkwy.
Fortune Drive
Fountain Plam Drive
Foxpoint Lane
Frederick Lane
Frederick Wy.
Fremont Court
Fremont Drive
Fremont Lane
Fremont Place
Fringe Drive
Furgol Lane

G

Garnet Drive
Garvey Drive
Gatewood Court
Gatewood Drive
Gauge Drive
Gem Lane
Gemini Drive
Gemini Place
Genoa Drive
George Lane E
Geronimo Blvd.
Geronimo Lane N
Geronimo Lane S
Gleneagles Drive
Glengarry Court
Glengarry Drive
Glengarry Place
Glorietta Drive
Glorietta Lane

Gold Dust Circle
Gold Dust Drive
Gold Dust Lane
Gold Springs Road
Goose Lane
Granada Lane
Green Acres Drive
Green Drive
Green Lane
Green Meadows Drive
Green Place
Greentree Drive
Grelle Street
Griffith Drive
Guest Lane
Gypsy Drive
Gypsy Lane

H

Hacienda Circle
Hacienda Court
Hacienda Drive
Hacienda Place
Hackberry Drive
Hagen Drive
Hagen Way
Hardrock Drive
Harrah Way
Harris Drive
Hassayampa Drive
Hataras Lane
Havasu Garden Drive
Havasupaid Blvd.
Havasupai Court
Hawk Lane
Hawkeye Drive
Hawkeye Plaza

Heine Street
Herbert Lane
Heron Lane
Hiawatha Drive
Hickory Drive
Hidden Valley Drive
Hidden Valley Lane
Highland Drive
Highlander Avenue
Highlander Lane
Highlander Plaza
Highlander Way
Hilldale Bay
Hilldale Drive
Hillington Lane
Hillside Drive
Hilltop Lane
Hillview Circle
Hillview Drive
Hillview Place
Hogan Lane
Holiday Drive
Hillister Drive
Hollister Lane
Holly Avenue
Hondo Lane
Honeybear Drive
Honeybee Drive
Hook Lane
Hopi Lane
Horzon Drive
Hornet Bay N
Hornet Bay S.
Hornet Drive
Horseshoe Canyon Drive
Horseshoe Canyon Lane

Horton Street
Hound Circle
Hound Drive
Hound Lane
Hound Place
Hubbel Drive
Hughes Lane
Hummingbird Drive
Hummingbird Lane
Hungry Horse Drive
Hunt Court
Hunter Lane
Huntington Drive
Huntington Place
Hurricane Drive
Hyde Park Avenue

I

Ibis Lane
Impala Lane
Imperial Way
Inca Drive
Inca Way
Indian Head Drive
Indian Hills Drive
Indian Land Drive
Indian Peak Drive
Indian Pipe Drive
Indian Pipe Lane
Indian Springs Drive
Industrial Blvd.
Injo Drive
Inlet Drive
Interceptor Drive
Interlake Drive
Inverness Circle
Inverness Court

Inverness Drive
Ironwood Drive
Iroquois Bay
Iroquois Circle
Iroquois Court
Iroquois Drive
Iroquois Lane
Iroquois Place
Iroquois Plaza
Islander Lane
Isle Cir Drive
Isleside Drive

J

Jacob Row
Jacob Row Circle
Jade Lane
Jaguar Lane
Jamaica blvd.
Jamaica Blvd. N
Jamaica Blvd. S
Jamaica Court
James Drive
Janet Drive
Jasper Drive
Javalina Lane
Jennie Lane
Jericho Drive
Jody Drive
Jolly Roger Drive
Jolly Roger Lane
Jones Drive
Jops Drive
Joshua Tree Drive
Joyce Lane

K

Kachina Lane

Kaibab Lane
Kearsage Drive
Kearsage Place
Keel Street
Keith Lane
Kenneth Lane
Kensington Drive
Kenwood Drive
Key Drive
Keywester Drive
Kibbey Drive
Kibbey Lane
Kickapoo
Kicking Horse Circle
Kicking Horse Court
Kicking Horse Drive
Kimo Circle
King Drive
Kingsbury Road
Kiowa Avenue
Kiowa Blvd.
Kiowa Blvd. S
Kiowa Circle
Kiowa Court
Kiowa Place
Kiowa Plaza
Kiowa Way.
Kirk Drive
Kitty hawk Drive
Kiva Circle
Kiva Drive
Klemm Drive
Knight Lane
Knobhill Lane
Knobhill Drive
Kootenay Drive

L

La Mesa Drive
La Paz Drive
Lafayette Lane
Lake Circle
Lake Drive
Lake Havasu Avenue N
Lake Havasu Avenue S
Lake Havasu Blvd. N
Lake Havasu Court
Lake Havasu Place
Lake Havasu Plaza
Lake Way
Lakeland Drive
Lakeland Lane
Lakeside Drive
Lakeview Road
Lempkin Drive
Lancer LANE
Landau Lane
Lantern Drive
Laramie Court
Laramie Drive
Laredo Lane
Largo Lane
Lark Lane
Lassen Lane
Latrelle Drive
Latrobe Drive
Latvia Lane
Lauren Lane
Laurie Lane
Lava Lane
Laverne Drive
Laverne Lane
Lear Bay
Leawood Drive

Lee Street
Lema Drive
Leonard Lane
Lera PLane
Library Lane
Lido Lane
Lighthouse Drive
Lightning Lane
Lilac Lane
Linda Drive
Linger Lane
Little Chief Drive
Little Drive
Little Finder Road
Little Finger Way
Little Plaza
Littler Lane
Llanos Dr
Labo Drive
Lockheed Bay
Locust Drive
Locust Lane
Lodestar Court
Lodestar Drive
Lodestar Lane
London Bridge Road
London Greens Lane
London Street
Longview Bay
Longivew Drive
Lookout Lane
Los Lagos Circle
Los Lagos Drive
Lost Dutchman Drive
Luna Que Pasa
Lunar Drive

M

Macaw Drive
Madera Drive
Magnolia Drive
Malahini Drive
Malahini Lane
Mallard Lane
Mandalay Drive
Mandalay Place
Mandarin Drive
Mangrum Drive
Manor Drive
Manor Lane
Manzanita Drive
Maracaibo Court
Maracaibo Drive
Maracaibo Lane
Maracaibo Way
Marauder Drive
Maricopa Avenue
Marina Road
Mariner Lane
Mariposa Drive
Marlboro Drive
Marlin Drive
Marshall Drive
Martinique Drive
Martinique Place
Mast Drive
Master Court
Matador Drive
Matador Lane
Mate Lane
Maverick Bay
Maverick Circle N
Maverick Circle S
Maverick Court

Maverick Drive
Maverick Lane
Maverick Place
Mayflower Street
McCulloch Bay
McCulloch Blvd. N
McCulloch Blvd. S
McCulloch Court
McCulloch Lane
McCulloch Place
Meadowlark Lane
Meadows Drive
Medicine Bow Drive
Mediterranean Lane
Melody Drive
Melrose Drive
Menking Street
Mercury Drive
Mesa Drive
Mescal Lane
Mescal Loop
Mescalaro Drive
Mesquite Ave
Meteor Lane
Metric Drive
Metz Lane
Mica Drive
Michael Drive
Milan Court
Milan Drive
Miller Lane
Mimosa Drive
Mimosa Lane
Minnow Lane
Minnow Place
Mirage Drive
Miramar Drive

Mission Drive N
Mission Drive S
Mission Plaza
Mission Way
Mitchell Lane
Moccasin Drive
Moccasin Lane
Mockingbird Drive
Mohican Drive
Mojave Drive
Molly Gibson Drive
Monaco Lane
Monazite Place
Monsoon Lane
Montana Vista
Monte Carlo Avenue
Monterey Drive
Montezuma Drive
Montrose Drive
Moonshine Drive
Morro Drive
Mountain View
Moyo Drive
MuCulloch Blvd. N
Mulberry Avenue
Mulberry Circle
Mulberry Lane
Murphy Drive
Mustand Drive

N

Naples Lane
Nassau Drive
Nautical Estates Drive
Nautilus Drive
Navajo Lane
Navigator Drive

Nelson Lane
Neptune Drive
Nero Lane
Newport Drive
Newport Lane
Nimrod Lane
Nolina Lane
Norris Court
Norris Drive
North Street
North View Drive
Northgate Road
Northstar Drive
Nottinghill Road
Nugget Court
Nugget Drive
Nugget Place

O

Oak Drive
Oakcreek Lane
Oakcreek Way
Oakridge Drive
Oakwood Drive
Oasis Drive
Oceanic Lane
Oconowoc Drive
Octillo Lane
Offshore Circle
Offshore Court
Ofshore Drive
Okeechobee Drive
Olive Lane
Oliver Lane
Onyx Lane
Opal Lane
Oppossum Drive

Orion Lane
Oro Grande Blvd.
Oro Grande Lane
Oro Grande Place
Oro Grande Plaza
Osage Court
Osage Drive
Osborn Drive
Osprey Lane
Ottawa Drive
Otter Lane
Outpost Drive
Outrigger Drive
Overland Drive
Own Drive
Oxford Road

P

Pacer Lane
Pacific Drive
Pacific Place
Packard Place
Packet Lane
Palace Way
Palisades Court
Palisades Drive
Palisades Lane
Palm Grove Drive
Palm Grove Way
Palmas Drive
Palmer Drive
Palmer Lane
Palo Verde Blvd. N
Palo Verde Blvd. S
Palo Verde Circle
Palo Verde Court
Palo Verde Lane

Palo Verde Place
Palo Verde Plaza
Palomino Drive
Papago Drive
Papago Lane
Papeete Drive
Papeete Place
Papoose drive
Papoose Lane
Park Avenue
Park Lane
Park Terrace Avenue
Park Terrace Bay
Park Terrace Court
Park Terrace Lane
Park Terrace Place
Parkview Drive
Partners Point
Pascaul Drive
Paseo del Sol
Paseo del Sol Avenue
Paseo Dorado
Paseo Granada
Paseo Verde
Paso de Oro Drive
Paso Drive
Patio Simpatico
Patrician Court
Patrician Drive
Petti Way
Pauite Place
Pauline Drive
Pawnee Drive
Pawnee Place
Peachblossom Drive
Pebble Beach
Pebble Drive

Peca Drive
Pelican Drive
Pelican Place
Pelican Plaza
Pena Lane
Pennant Lane
Penny Drive
Penny Lane
Pepperwood Circle
Pepperwood Drive
Perlite Lane
Pero Drive
Peruvian Drive
Peruvian Lane
Peruvian Place
Peruvian Plaza
Pheasant Lane
Phoenix Drive
Pierson Drive
Pima Drive N.
Pima Drive S.
Pima Square S.
Pin Drive
Pinal Lane
Pine Lane
Pinion Tree Drive
Pintail drive
Pioneer Drive
Piper Bay
Piper Drive
Piper Loop
Pirate Lane
Pitch Lane
Plan Tree Drive
Platte Drive
Player Lane
Plaza del Oro

Plaza del Plata
Plaza del Sol
Plaza Estrella
Plaza Granada
Plaza Hermosa
Plaza la Cresta
Plaza Lago
Plaza Laredo
Plaza Paloma
Plaza Roca
Plaza Verde
Plebe Lane
Pocahontas Drive
Polaris Drive
Pontchartrain Drive
Pony Circle
Pony Drive
Pony Lane
Pony Place
Poplar Drive
Poppy Lane
Poppy Trail Court
Poppy Trail Drive
Poppy Trail Place
Porpoise Drive
Port Drive
Poseidon Court
Poseidon Drive
Poseidon Lane
Poseidon Place
Powder Lane
Powderhorn Drive
Powell Drive
Powhattan Drive
Pram Lane
Precision Drive
Prestwick Drive

Price Drive
Prickly Pear Street
Princess drive
Privateer Drive
Pueblo Drive
Putt Lane

Q

Quail Lane
Quail Ridge Drive
Quartz Lane
Quartzite Lane
Queens Bay
Querio Drive

R

Rainbow Avenue N.
Rainbow Avenue S.
Rainbow Court
Rainbow Lane
Rainbow Place
Ramrod Lane
Ranchero Drive
Ranchero Lane
Ranchito Drive
Rango Circle
Rango Drive
Rango Place
Rapier Lane
Ravello Drive
Ravello Lane
Ravello Place
Raven Lane
Red Cloud Drive
Red drive
Red Lane
Red Rock Drive
Reef Drive

Regal Court
Regal Drive
Regal Lane
Regatta Court
Regatta Drive
Regency Drive
Reimer Drive
Reservation Drive
Reseorter Drive
Resorter Lane
Revere drive
Ridgeview Drive
Riverbelle Drive
Riverboat Drive
Riverside Drive
Riviera Blvd.
Riviera Drive
Roadrunner Drive
Roamer Lane
Roanoke Drive
RobinLane
Rock Lane
Rocking Horse Drive
Rolling Hills Drive
Rolling Hills Plaza N.
Roundup Drive
Rover Drive
Ruby Lane
Rudolph Drive
Runabout Drive
Russel Drive
Rustler Drive

S

Sabino Drive
Saddleback Bay
Saddleback Drive

Sage Brush Street
Sage Lane
Saguaro Drive
Sahara Drive
Sail Lane
Sailing Hawks Drive
Saint Claire Drive
Salem Lane
Salter Drive
San Juan Drive
San Juan Lane
San Pan Lane
San Dab Court
San Dab Drive
San Dab Place
San Dab Plaza
Sandpiper Drive
Sandwood Court
Sandwood Drive
Sandwood Place
Sandy Drive
Sapphire Street
Sara Parkway
Sarasota Drive
Saratoga Avenue
Saratoga Court
Satellite Court
Satellite Drive
Saturn Lane
Scott Drive
Scout Drive
Sea Ace Lane
Sea Angler Court
Sea Angler Drive
Sea Knight Drive
Sea Lancer Drive
Sea Queen Drive

Sea Queen Place
Sea Swallow Drive
Sea Venture Drive
Seabring Court
Seabring Drive
Sedona Drive
Segawa Lane
Seminole Lane
Seneca Lane
Senita Bay
Senita Drive
Senita Lane
Sentinel Drive
Serenidad Vereda
Seville Lane
Shasta Lane
Shawnee Lane
Shearwater Lane
Sheik Drive
Shiawassee Drive
Shorewood Circle
Shorewood Court
Shorewood Drive
Shorewood Place
Shorewood Plaza
Shoshone Court
Shoshone Drive
Shoshone Lane
ShoShone Place
Shoshone Plaza
Shultz Street
Silver Arrow Circle
Silver Arrow Court
Silver Arrow Drive
Silver Clipper Lane
Silver King Drive
Silver Saddle Bay

Silver Saddle Drive
Silverado Drive
Silverbell Drive
Silversmith Bay
Silversmith Drive
Silverspoon Drive
Simitan Drive
Simitan Lane
Sinbad Lane
Sioux Lane
Siracco Drive
Site Six Road
Skagit Lane
Skimmer Lane
Skipper Lane
Slice Lane
Sloop Court
Sloop Drive
Sloop Lane
Smoketree Avenue N
Smoketree Avenue S
Smokey Drive
Snead Circle
Snead Drive
Snipe Lane
Snow Bird Drive
Solar Bay
Solar Circle
Solar Court
Solar Drive
Sombrero Drive
Sorrel Lane
Sorrento Lane
Sotol Lane
Souchak Drive
Southweater Lane
Southwind Avenue

Southwind Lane
Southwind Place
Spawr Circle
Spezzano Way
Spirit Lane
Sponson Drive
Spring Lane
Sprite Lane
Spruce Drive
Squall King Court
Squall King Drive
Squall King Place
Squaw Drive
Squaw Way
Stallion Lane
Stanford Court
Stanford Drive
Star Drive
Stardust Bay
Stardust Drive
Stardust Place
Starfish Drive
Starline Drive
Starlite Lane
Starmist Lane
Stephen View Drive
Stingray Lane
Stone Acre Drive
Stonebridge Lane
Stonecrop Drive
Stratford Street
Stroke Drive
Sturgeon Drive
Sumac Drive
Sumerset Drive
Sun Chief Lane
Sunchaser Lane

Sunfield drive
Sunfish Lane
Sunflower Drive
Sunkentree Drive
Sunkentree Lane
Sunliner Lane
Sunny Point Drive
Sunny Ridge Circle
Sunny Ridge Drive
Sunray Drive
Sunset Drive
Sunshine Drive
Supai Drive
Surf Lane
Surf Song Lane
Surfrider Lane
Surrey Hills Lane
Surrey Lane
Sutton Place
Suzie Lane
Swanee Lane
Swanson Avenue
Swanson Plaza
Sweetgrass Drive
Sweetwater Avenue
Sweetwater Lane
Swift Drive
Swift Way
Swilcan Bridge Road
Swirl Drive
Swordfish Drive
Sycamore Place
Sycamore Way

T

Tahiti Lane
Tahitian Circle

Tahitian Court
Tahitian Drive
Tahitian Place
Tahoe Lane
Tail Star Lane
Talisman Drive
Talisman Lane
Talley Drive
Talley Lane
Tamarack Drive
Tampico
Tanglewood Court
Tanglewood Drive
Tanglewood Lane
Tanglewood Place
Tanqueray Drive
Taos Lane
Tarpon Drive
Tarpon Drive N.
Tarpon Plaza
Taurus Lane
Teal Lane
Tecumseh Drive
Ted Lane
Tee Drive
Tee Lane
Tee Place
Teetsa Lane
Tehachapi Drive
Tema Drive
Tempest Lane
Texoma Drive
Thundercloud Drive
Thistle Drive
Thistle Lane
Thrasher Drive
Thunderbird Drive

Westminister Road
Westport Drive
Whaler Court
Whaler Drive
Whirlwind Lane
White Oak Drive
Whitecap Circle
Whitecap Court
Whitecap Drive
Widgeon Drive
Widgeon Lane
Wigwam Drive
William Drive
Willow Avenue
Wilson Drive
Window Rock drive
Window Rock Plaza
Window Rock Road
Windsor Beach Road
Windward Lane
Wings Loop
Winifred Circle
Winifred Place
Winifred Way
Winnebago Drive
Winnebago Lane
Winston Circle
Winston Court
Winston Drive
Winston place
Winterhaven Court
Winterhaven Drive
Wolf Lane
Wood Lane
Wrangler Lane
Weren Lane

Aerial view of Lake Havasu City and Lake Havasu
(Credit: LHCPROPERTIES.COM)

Y

Yaqui Drive
Yaqui Lane
Yattahhey Drive
Yavapai Way
Yazoo Circle
Yazoo Court
Yazoo Drive
Yazoo Lane
Yonder Drive
Yosemite Court

Yosemite Drive
Yosemite Trail
Yucca Drive
Yucca Lane
Yucca Plaza
Yuma Drive

Made in the USA
Las Vegas, NV
14 July 2021